Millie's Life Lessons:

Adventures in Trusting God

A Study Guide Based on
Books One and Two of the
A Life of Faith: Millie Keith Series

Written by
Wendy Witherow
and Beverly Elliott

MCP
Mission City Press
Franklin, Tennessee

Cover & Interior Design:	Richmond & Williams, Nashville, Tennessee
Cover Photography:	Michelle Grisco Photography, West Covina, California
Typesetting:	BookSetters, White House, Tennessee

Unless otherwise indicated, all Scripture references are from the Holy Bible, New International Version (NIV). Copyright © 1973, 1978, 1984, by International Bible Society. Used by permission of Zondervan Publishing House, Grand Rapids, MI. All rights reserved. Note: Where there are italics within a verse of Scripture, it is emphasis added by the authors of this study guide.

Millie Keith and *A Life of Faith* are trademarks of Mission City Press, Inc.

For more information, write to Mission City Press at P.O. Box 681913, Franklin, Tennessee 37068-1913, or visit our web site at:

www.alifeoffaith.com

Library of Congress Catalog Card Number: 2002103831
Mission City Press
Millie's Life Lessons: Adventures in Trusting God
ISBN #: 1-928749-57-7

Printed in the United States of America
1 2 3 4 5 6 7 8 — 06 05 04 03 02

Table of Contents

Introduction

Why Center a Bible Study Around a Fictional Character?

A passionate desire to be faithful to God. Honesty and eagerness to know more about God and His ways. Striving to overcome personal weaknesses and reflect the love of Jesus Christ. Facing life's challenges and adventures with courage, integrity, and determination. These are just a few of the endearing characteristics that make the literary character of Millie Keith an appropriate subject for a Bible study.

Written by Miss Martha Finley (author of the best-selling *Elsie Dinsmore* series) and originally published in 1876 as the *Mildred Keith* series, the story of the life and spiritual commitment of Millie Keith is not only relevant but refreshing to girls of today. Although Millie's integrity of heart captures our attention, Millie is far from perfect (unlike her famous cousin Elsie Dinsmore), and it is her willingness to *grow* into maturity that readers most admire. As we enter the life and times of Millie Keith, we make the journey of growing closer to God right alongside her. In the end, we are personally challenged and inspired to make faithfulness to God the goal of our own lives and to allow our Master Potter to mold and shape us. Yet this process requires that we learn to trust Him.

Millie's Life Lessons: Adventures in Trusting God is an in-depth workbook designed to teach the crucial life skill of trusting God. We use the life experiences of Millie Keith to do that because Millie is so easy to relate to. She is a Christian heroine who clearly demonstrates the timeless virtues of all those who daily strive to live a life of faith so that God might advance His Kingdom through us. We trust Him because He is trust*worthy*!

First Things First

In order to trust and follow God, we must know Him and have His Holy Spirit living inside us. If you have not yet accepted Jesus as your Savior, you can do so right now. It is as simple as saying a prayer to God and believing in the Lord with all your heart. You can say it in your own words, or you can pray the following simple prayer, either alone or with another Christian:

Dear Heavenly Father, I know that I am a sinner and have often done things that are wrong. I am sorry for my sins and I pray that You will forgive me for all of them. I accept the free gift of Jesus' death on the Cross in my place. I believe that Jesus died for my sins and was raised from the dead. I invite You and Your Holy Spirit to come live inside my heart. I give my life to You right now, and I ask that from this day forth, You would help me to love You, to trust and follow You, to walk in Your ways, and to get to know You better. It is in Jesus' name that I pray these things. Amen.

If you prayed to accept Jesus, welcome to the family of God! Now you can look forward to a wonderful relationship with God! Tell someone else (preferably another Christian) about the commitment you just made, and if that someone else is not your parent, then you should also tell your mother or father or guardian.

How to Use This Study Guide

Before Beginning Your Study

*T*he questions in this workbook are based on plots and subplots from the first two books of the "A Life of Faith: Millie Keith" series. Therefore we strongly recommend that you read both *Millie's Unsettled Season* (book one) and *Millie's Courageous Days* (book two) prior to beginning this study. You will find brief portions from these two novels quoted throughout the study to remind you of Millie's adventures, but this cannot substitute for being familiar with the characters and storylines. And you will enjoy knowing Millie more fully having read the first two novels.

Studying Millie's Life Lessons

*W*hen starting a new Bible study, it's easy to get excited and rush through the lessons. But this study guide is not designed for you to sit down and read cover to cover. Remember that the object of your study is to learn to know and trust God. This takes time. To get the most out of this study, we encourage you to move slowly. We hope that you will progress through *Millie's Life Lessons* gradually, with careful thought and prayer.

As you embark on *Millie's Life Lessons*, remember that your goal is not to finish the study quickly, but to "be transformed by the renewing of your mind," as Romans 12:2 encourages us. Each chapter in this study guide has five lessons. *Do not attempt to complete a whole chapter in one day.* Instead, do each lesson slowly, one at a time. It's important not to skip any of the learning activities. We have purposefully chosen each question and assignment to help you understand and apply God's truths to your life. So pace yourself—

try not to do more than one lesson a day. By taking your time, you will allow the truths to inspire your thoughts, penetrate your heart, and influence your actions. And when that happens, real change takes place in your heart.

Throughout this course, you will find that the only way for you to become more like Jesus is to grow in your love for Him.

As you begin your own adventures in trusting God, remember that what you're doing is much more than just answering questions or looking up Scripture verses. Try not to look at this as just filling in the answers—look at it as encountering God! *Expect to experience Him.* Much prayer went into the design and content of this study. Our hope is that you will meet heart-to-heart with your Creator—the One who loves you and has great things for your life! With each question and assignment, look for Him and listen to what He is personally saying to you. If you get stuck or need help understanding something, do not be reluctant to ask your parents, your youth leader, or a Christian friend. As Millie learned, God often speaks to us through other people. Also, we have intentionally included some words in this study guide that might be a challenge to you. *Keep a dictionary handy so that you can learn the meanings of new words!* But most importantly, know that God wants to speak to you—just be willing to take your time and listen!

This is *your* book. Be open and honest with your answers. Feel free to write in the margins, to jot down additional ideas, and to make a note of questions that may come to mind. Use additional sheets of paper if you find that you need more room to write.

It is very important that you seek to *apply* the principles you will learn in this study guide to your everyday life. To help you, we have included some symbols at the end of each chapter to remind you to *stop and digest what you have learned.*

When you see this symbol, pause and look back over the chapter. Ask the Holy Spirit to show you the most important things He wants you to remember. Put a star beside those truths. Then, in your own words, summarize what He showed you.

When you see this symbol, rewrite your thoughts as a prayer, asking God to help you grow and apply the truths He's taught you throughout the chapter.

Scripture Memory: From God's Heart to Yours

If you're familiar with the *Millie Keith* novels, then you know that Millie memorized many Scriptures. Time after time God reminded Millie of a certain verse that gave her wisdom, peace, or hope for whatever situation she found herself in. Millie was young, but she was already becoming anchored in God's Word. She knew the importance of hiding God's Word in her heart, and as a result, she was a very mature Christian for her young age.

We want you to follow Millie's lead and begin to make Scripture memory a part of your life. The Bible says that "faith comes from hearing the message, and the message is heard through the word of Christ" (Romans 10:17). This truth is quite simple: To increase your faith in God, read the Word and hide it in your heart!

When you memorize God's Word, you are essentially storing up powerful and priceless treasures in your heart. God will use His Word to strengthen you and give you hope. As with Millie, God will recall His Word from your heart and mind in moments of hardship, trouble, or unease. God's Word equips you for all of life's adventures. His Word endures forever—the Word will not rust away or grow old and useless. Instead, it will continually bring life to your soul, sustaining you all the days of your life.

For this reason, we've included learning Scriptures "by heart" in *Millie's Life Lessons*.

This large heart symbol will mark the memory verse for each chapter. Work on memorizing the verse before, during, and after you read the chapter.

This small heart symbol will mark the memory verse for the entire study guide, Proverbs 3:5–6. Work on memorizing it and testing yourself on how well you remember it throughout all of *Millie's Life Lessons*.

Some of the memory verses will be short and fairly easy to memorize; others will be more difficult. But TAKE YOUR TIME. Scripture memory is well worth the investment of time you put into it!

At the end of this book, we have included Scripture Memory Cards that you can use as a helpful resource. Here are some suggestions for how to use them:

❖ Remove the cards from the back of this book and use them as flash cards.

- ❖ Study one card at a time.

- ❖ Read the verse and think about the meaning. Make sure you understand *all* the words in the text. Think about how it applies to you. Ask others (such as your parents or youth leader or a Christian friend) what they think God is saying in the verse.

- ❖ Make a sign with the verse written on it and hang it in full view where you spend time or will see it each day—near your bed, at your desk, on the refrigerator, or elsewhere.

- ❖ Carry the verse card with you. Recite the verse out loud several times throughout the day. Do this while riding in the car, waiting in line, during breaks at school, etc.

- ❖ Quiz yourself until you can recite the verse without looking.

- ❖ Recite the verse to a parent or friend until you have it completely memorized.

- ❖ Wait until one verse is committed to memory before moving on to the next.

- ❖ With each new verse you study, do not neglect the ones you've already memorized. Continue reciting and quizzing yourself on each verse you learned.

- ❖ Think about these verses as you speak, act, and make decisions. Ask God to help you to live these truths in everything you do.

- ❖ If you can, find someone (a parent or friend) who will memorize verses along with you. Then you can help each other!

The greatest blessing of Scripture memory is this: God wants to personally speak to you through His Word. As you step out in trust and hide His Word in your heart, God will touch you in a personal way, making the ancient Scriptures relevant to your own life. There's no real way to describe the thrill of encountering God—you just have to experience it for yourself. Ask Him, *What do You want me to learn from this Scripture today, Lord?* And expect an answer. He will show you!

Last Words

*A*s we will learn, Aunt Wealthy helped Millie to see that life with God is a grand adventure. Our hope for you is that you will begin to see your own life with God as an exciting adventure—one that is vibrant and fun and full of your own *life lessons* that you can share with others. By sharing those lessons with your friends, you can even impact your own generation for God's Kingdom!

As you learn God's Word and discover more about trusting God through *Millie's Life Lessons,* our prayer is that you will enjoy this study and enjoy growing closer to God. We

urge you to invest in your relationship with the Lord more than you invest in any other relationship. You will find that when you give God your time and your heart, He will give back much, much more!

An exciting journey of going deeper with the Lord begins right now. Put your trust in Him. Welcome Him into more areas of your heart and life. If you're not sure how, don't worry. Millie learned step by step, and so can you!

Jeremiah 33:3 says, "Call to me and I will answer you and tell you great and unsearchable things you do not know." Pause for a moment to pray and ask the Lord to teach you great and unsearchable things that you do not know during the study of *Millie's Life Lessons*. You can be sure that it is a prayer He will answer as you work through this study guide!

Now, if you are ready to begin, take some time to memorize Proverbs 3:5–6, the key verse for this entire study guide. Be sure you have memorized it "by heart" before moving on to the first chapter. Once you have memorized it, we will begin the study together. May *Millie's Life Lessons* greatly enhance your walk with and love for our beloved Savior!

Trust in the LORD with all your heart
and lean not on your own understanding;
in all your ways acknowledge him,
and he will make your paths straight.

PROVERBS 3:5–6

CHAPTER

Life is an Adventure

Lesson 1
Trusting God

Lesson 2
Straight Paths

Lesson 3
Tea Parties & Wild Adventures

Lesson 4
Embracing Change

Lesson 5
Let Go & Let God

Life is an Adventure

by heart

$\mathcal{D}$o not let your hearts be troubled. Trust in God; trust also in me.   —JOHN 14:1

Trusting God

"$\mathcal{O}$h, Aunt Wealthy," Millie cried, as Wealthy's boot touched solid ground. "It's decided!"

"My child, what is it?" asked the older lady, dropping the letter to take the girl's hand and draw her to a seat on the sofa. "What is decided?"

Millie spoke with a determined effort to be calm.

"This morning at breakfast, Pappa told us—us children, I mean—he and Mamma had talked it over last night, and you know they have been praying about it, and…"

"And?" Wealthy clasped Millie's hand to her heart.

"We are going to move . . . to . . . to . . . Pleasant Plains, Indiana."

"The frontier!" Wealthy gasped, sinking back on the couch.

"Just as soon as we can get ready. Isn't it marvelous?" Millie said, and burst into tears.

— From *Millie's Unsettled Season*, page 5

Welcome to *Millie's Life Lessons: Adventures in Trusting God!*

$\mathcal{W}$hen we meet twelve-year-old Millie Keith for the first time in *Millie's Unsettled Season* (book one), her life has just been turned upside down by some exciting but very upsetting news. She and her family will be leaving Lansdale, Ohio, Millie's hometown since her birth, and moving to Pleasant Plains, Indiana. From a charming, beautiful, prosperous, and established city, to a "rough and undeveloped" town on the wide-open frontier!

As Millie discovered, trusting God isn't always easy. But it is always exciting! God had special plans for Millie Keith, and the accomplishment of those plans required that Millie trust Him.

Do you know that God has special plans for *your* life, too? They are plans born out of God's heart of love. Plans you cannot imagine. Plans full of experiences too marvelous for words! But just like in Millie's case, the accomplishment of God's plans for your life requires that you trust Him too.

That is why we have written this study guide—to help you learn to trust God. Learning to trust God is like beginning on an exciting journey. We want to share part of that journey with you, and help you learn some important lessons now that will save you from some heartache and benefit you for the rest of your life. That's what "life lessons" are all about!

So, let's get started.

First and foremost, in order to trust God you must know Him. If you have not yet met Jesus Christ and asked Him to save you from your sins, it is something that you need to do. A relationship with Jesus will set the whole course of your life going in the right direction, and it is the foundation for everything we are going to teach in this study guide. We discussed this in the Introduction under the section called "First Things First." Read that section now if you have not done so already.

Once you have asked Jesus into your heart, the goal is to get to know Him better. When Millie gave her heart to Jesus, she got into the habit of praying and reading her Bible every day. These things helped her get to know the Lord better. Although she wasn't there yet, she sought to trust God in ALL circumstances—even during the most unsettling of seasons!

 **It takes courage to trust in God because you can't see Him. But the better you know Him, the easier it will be for you to trust Him.**

To trust God, you must:

❖ understand what it means to trust

❖ know God's nature and character—especially His goodness and faithfulness

❖ have a new mindset—the mindset of a "pioneer for God"

❖ know how to hear God's voice and be led by His Holy Spirit

❖ be able to manage your emotions and conquer your bad attitudes

❖ know how to see through eyes of faith, and

❖ let God guide you in your relationships.

Let's look at our memory verse for this whole study guide, Proverbs 3:5–6. Complete the missing words below.

_____ in the Lord with all your _____ and lean not on your own

_____; in all your ways _____ him, and he

will make your paths _____.

In your own words, describe what you think it means to "trust" God.

God began a work in Millie's heart when it was decided that the Keiths would move to Pleasant Plains. This was an area of Millie's life where God asked her to trust Him. Millie had to leave her friends and everything that was familiar to her, and she had to leave behind certain expectations that she had about her future. Everything seemed uncertain as she packed up and moved away. Millie had to trust God in a deeper way.

Can you think of some areas of your life where God might be asking you to trust Him in a deeper way? If so, list them below. Be specific.

How do you feel about the idea of trusting God? At this point in your life, does trusting God seem to come easily for you or do you find it difficult?

Let's look at the definition of "trust" from the dictionary.

Trust means:

❖ to place confidence in, depend on, rely on

❖ to commit or place in one's care or keeping, to entrust

❖ to permit to stay or go or to do something without fear or misgiving

❖ to rely on the truthfulness or accuracy of, to believe, to hope or expect confidently.

Look back at John 14:1, our memory verse for this chapter, and write it out here:

Find the word *troubled* in a dictionary and write the definition here:

Based on that definition, what do you think it means to have a troubled heart?

Can you think of a recent time when you had a troubled heart? If so, describe it in the space below.

Troubled and *trust* seem like opposites, don't they? Notice that in Proverbs 3:5–6, you are told to trust in the Lord "with *all* your heart." Do you think this is possible when your heart is troubled? Why or why not?

Nahum 1:7 tells us, "The Lord is good, a refuge in times of trouble. He cares for those who trust in him." This is a promise you can count on!

Straight Paths

The girlish figure who slipped out the back door of the stately brick home in the center of town didn't seem to notice the whisper of spring. She clutched a large, well-worn book to her chest, closed her eyes and leaned her head against the door.

Trust in the Lord…

"Millie!" A child's voice called, "Millie? Where are you?"

"Oh, not now!" Millie protested and ran across the garden to a fragrant cave beneath the arching lilacs. When she was sure that no one could see her behind the curtain of purple blooms, she sat down and opened the book.

"You know I am trying to acknowledge You, Lord," she prayed out loud. "But has there been a mistake? Something has gone wrong this time. I'm sure it has. Remember the verse Mamma gave me just yesterday? You must remember it, it's in *Your* book!" She flipped the Bible open. "Proverbs 3:5—"

—From *Millie's Unsettled Season*, page 3

In the excerpt for this lesson, we learn that Millie was making a diligent effort to "acknowledge" God in her life. What does it mean to *acknowledge* God? It means:

❖ to recognize Him and believe that He exists

❖ to look attentively at Him with reverence and esteem

❖ to admit that He is the One who governs your life and the lives of all people, and

❖ to yield to Him.

Acknowledging God is the basis for our faith as believers. Hebrews 11:6 says, "And without faith it is impossible to please God, because anyone who comes to him must *believe that he exists* and that he rewards those who earnestly seek him."

 **The first step in your faith is acknowledging God, which includes believing that God exists and admitting that He has the right to govern the lives of all people—including you.**

When we truly acknowledge God, we *want* to seek Him. We want to commit and turn every one of our "ways"—every aspect of our lives, including every thought, desire, decision, and plan—over to Him. We want to serve and follow Him. "I have considered my ways and have turned my steps to your statutes," said David in Psalm 119:59.

Acknowledging God in all our ways is a requirement (a condition) for many of God's promises.

 **With many of God's promises, there is a response of love and obedience required on your part.**

God will never force us to love Him or obey Him. These are always our choices. But when we do, we open a spiritual floodgate for all the promises and blessings of God to be accomplished in our lives.

Proverbs 3:5–6, our memory verse for this workbook, contains one such promise. Fill in the blank spaces below to see the promise:

Trust in the LORD with all your heart and lean not on your own understanding; in_____

your ways acknowledge him, and he will _____.

Acknowledging God in all her ways was important to Millie because she wanted Him to make her paths straight! But when Millie received the news about Pleasant Plains, it didn't seem to her like her family was on a very straight path. Rather, Millie was sure there must have been a mistake and now they were headed down a crooked and uncertain path.

Have you ever walked on a crooked path — a path that had many obstacles on it, like weeds, overgrown roots, or rocks and holes? Perhaps you've even twisted your ankle on such a path. But a straight path, on the other hand, does not leave you encumbered or slow you down. Your feet are secure and you reach your destination with much more ease. Do you know that you are on a path right now? Your journey through life is like being on a path, and IF you acknowledge God on the way, He offers to make your paths straight, helping you avoid the pitfalls of a crooked path.

> Commit your way to the LORD; trust in him and he will do this: He will make your righteousness shine like the dawn, the justice of your cause like the noonday sun. (Psalm 37:5–6)

Acknowledging God in every aspect of life was not only important to Millie, it was important to her parents as well. Millie's parents believed that guiding all of their children toward a relationship with God was essential to their walking a straight path as individuals and as a family. We see this in the following statements:

"My husband is a Christian man," Marcia said. "And from the very first day of our marriage we have been determined that our household will follow the Lord."

— From *Millie's Unsettled Season*, page 129

After his prayer, Stuart said, "That is the kind of individuals I asked God to make us, and the kind of home I want to have. 'As for me and my household, we will serve the LORD,' " said Stuart, quoting Joshua 24:15.

— From *Millie's Courageous Days*, page 51

Joshua 24:15 tells us that we need to *choose* who we are going to serve. Millie's parents made strong statements about their desire for their family to follow God in every area of their lives. When you determine for yourself to follow the Lord in all the areas of your

life, you too are acknowledging God "in all your ways" and making a statement of your own faith in God.

Take a few minutes to think about your own commitment to the Lord. Do you want to acknowledge Him in all your ways? If so, make a statement of your faith and commitment and write it below:

MY STATEMENT OF FAITH AND COMMITMENT

Your statement of faith and commitment is a way of acknowledging God. And remember what Proverbs 3:6 says about that? It says that if you acknowledge Him in all your ways, God will make your paths straight!

 **A straight path is one that is headed somewhere and has a sure destiny at the end. God wants you to walk on the straight path He has prepared for you.**

There are many blessings that accompany a straight path. The Hebrew origin of the word *straight* actually means "right, pleasant, prosperous, good, upright, and even." Remember the Israelites who wandered aimlessly in the wilderness? God was not able to lead them straight into the Promised Land because in their hearts they did not acknowledge Him. Do you want to wander aimlessly in life? Or would you rather be on a straight path that will take you where you need to go?

It's important to remember that a straight path isn't always easy. After all, even a steep path can be straight. But with God's leading, it will be easy to follow the path He sets before you. You can be assured that it will be a solid path to put your feet on.

Look up Psalm 37:23–24 and complete the missing words in the verse below:

If the LORD _____ in a man's way, he makes his steps _____; though he

_____, he will not fall, for the LORD _____ him with his _____.

 **You may stumble on your straight path with God, but God will not let you fall!**

In contrast, read what God has to say about the wicked: "The path of the righteous is like the first gleam of dawn, shining ever brighter till the full light of day. But the way of the wicked is like deep darkness; they do not know what makes them stumble" (Proverbs 4:18–19). And in Proverbs 2:15, we are told that the wicked walk on crooked paths.

God desires to accompany you on your own adventures in trusting Him! As you begin to trust Him more and more, acknowledging Him in all your ways, He will indeed guide you along straight paths.

In the space below, describe what the path of YOUR life has looked like by circling the answer that best fits. It may have started out crooked and then straightened out when you met Jesus. Or maybe you feel like it is still an aimless, wandering path. If this is the case, know that God can make the crooked paths straight (see Luke 3:5).

1. The path of my life has been [straight   crooked   slightly curvy]

2. I have made [good   unwise   sometimes bad] choices about obeying my parents, choosing my friends, and maintaining the attitudes of my heart.

3. The line that represents my answer in number 1 looks like this: [draw your path in the space below]

In conclusion, take comfort in these promises:

Isaiah 42:16 — I will lead the blind by ways they have not known, along unfamiliar paths I will guide them; I will turn the darkness into light before them and make the rough places smooth. These are the things I will do; I will not forsake them.

Isaiah 26:7 — The path of the righteous is level; O upright One, you make the way of the righteous smooth.

Now take a few moments to pray and ask the Lord to guide you and make your paths straight. Ask Him to help you acknowledge Him in ALL your ways.

Tea Parties & Wild Adventures

"It isn't what we fear, is it, Millie?" Annabeth said. "It can't be. We've all been praying and praying…"

Millie's eyes stung, but she blinked hard. "My father and mother have been praying too, and they decided…the opportunities are just so good in Indiana…"

"Indiana!" Camilla collapsed in a heap on the ottoman. "Not possible. You can't! There should be a law against it!"

"A law against the Keiths moving to Indiana?" Bea shook her head.

"Of course not," Camilla said. "A law against the Keiths leaving Lansdale at all. I think we should sign a petition!"

"Annabeth, dear, are you quite all right?" Wealthy was looking at the tall, quiet girl.

Bea and Camilla stopped their chatter.

"We've always been together," Annabeth said. "How can you leave?"

Millie's throat felt tight. Even if she could have spoken, there was no word to express all the feelings jumbled inside. Not one word.

—From *Millie's Unsettled Season*, page 17

John 14:1, our memory verse for this chapter, says, "Do not let your hearts be troubled. Trust in God; trust also in me."

One thing that will help us trust in God is to learn a simple principle that Aunt Wealthy referred to in a conversation with Millie.

 **Life is an adventure.**

> "How could this possibly be good?" Millie asked [distressed about her circumstances].
>
> . . . Millie put her hands over her face, but Aunt Wealthy's arms went around her instantly. . . . "God calls us to a wild adventure, not a tea party, my dear," [said Aunt Wealthy].
>
> —From *Millie's Courageous Days*, pages 16–17

Aunt Wealthy saw life as a wild *adventure.* And she loved adventures!

When you hear the words "wild adventure," what picture comes to your mind?

When you hear the words "tea party," what do you picture?

Adventures are experiences that are exciting, uncertain, risky, and unpredictable. They are experiences that are never boring and always stretch you, usually well beyond what you are comfortable with.

Tea parties, on the other hand, are very predictable. Girls dress up in their prettiest clothes and have tea and sandwiches and cookies together. It is a sweet and charming time, which everyone enjoys—a time away from the cares and difficulties of life.

When Aunt Wealthy said "God calls us to a wild adventure, not a tea party," she was teaching Millie to see life as an adventure.

Pause and think for a minute. Do you like adventures? Why or why not?

If you see life as a tea party, when difficulties, troubles, changes, or challenges come (and they will come!), you will be disappointed and confused, thinking of them as *unwanted intruders* on your happiness. "It's not supposed to be this way," you'll probably say or feel.

But is life really supposed to be trouble-free? In the sixteenth chapter of the book of John, Jesus told His disciples that times of great turmoil and difficulty would come. But in John 16:33, He went on to say, "I have told you these things, so that in me you may have peace. In this world you will have trouble. But take heart! I have overcome the world."

 **In the adventure of life, we should *expect* challenges, changes, difficulties, and troubles to come. That's what makes life an adventure!**

If you are a Christian, there are two promises in John 16:33 that you can cling to when you have troubles of any kind:

1. In Christ, you can have *peace* in the midst of your troubles.

2. Through Christ, you can be an *overcomer*, which means that God will get you through the trial and you will be a better, stronger person because of it.

 **We do not need to fear when challenges, changes, difficulties, and troubles come. Because of the promises we have through Christ, our trials can now become adventures that we can embrace and accept, rather than dread and fear.**

Many people in the Bible (for example, Noah) had "adventures." Can you name some of the people and their adventures?

List some character traits that you think these Bible people must have had to face their own adventures with God.

NAME	Noah			
ADVENTURE	Building the Ark			
CHARACTER TRAITS	persistence diligence faithfulness obedience patience			

You may have listed courage, obedience, honesty, and a deep love for God. But one of the biggest traits these men and women must have had was TRUST in God! It's so important that we trust God if we are going to live our lives for Him. Without trust in God, we probably won't get very far in an adventure with Him!

When we meet Millie at the start of *Millie's Unsettled Season*, she was beginning to see that God wasn't calling her to a cozy tea party. He was inviting her to join Him in a grand adventure. Millie knew that she would have to trust God in a greater way if she was going to get through all the changes that were heading in her direction.

Do you have any new changes or challenges heading your way? Are you entering a new grade at school, moving to a new city, trying out for a sport, joining an extracurricular activity for the first time, or taking on new responsibilities at home? Write them here and think about the challenges these changes might bring.

How can you look at these changes as an adventure with God?

What character traits would you like to grow stronger in to prepare you for your adventures with God?

"But I trust in you, O LORD; I say, 'You are my God.' My times are in your hands" (Psalm 31:14–15).

Embracing Change

"Why, I remember," the tiny lady said, "when God changed my adventure. I was having a wonderful time living in a small room in Boston, helping servants just out of their indentures to find work, and teaching them to read the Scriptures. I was sure I would spend my whole life working with the Ladies Aid Society. Then I received word that my beloved sister's husband had died, and she herself was ill. I hurried home to care for her and her two-year-old daughter, but she was taken home to the Lord. As you can imagine, I was heartbroken and confused. My whole life had to change. I found myself with a child to raise—your mother. And look at what the Lord has done! A spinster like me, with a niece as dear as a daughter and eight just-as-good-as grandchildren. God had a very special plan."

"Well, I *thought* He had one for me," Millie said. "Maybe I did something wrong and He changed His mind!"

"Nonsense," Aunt Wealthy said. "He isn't just sending the Keith clan. He is sending His very own Millie Keith, the bravest, most outspoken girl I know. There must be something very special He wants you to do in Pleasant Plains. Come along."

—From *Millie's Unsettled Season*, pages 6–7

God had a plan for Aunt Wealthy—a plan that changed her whole life! Now Millie was questioning God's plan for her own life. Millie thought that her life was headed in a certain direction—finish her schooling in Lansdale, attend college with her best friend, and then explore the world and accomplish something grand! But God had other plans for Millie — plans that began with a move to Pleasant Plains.

Aunt Wealthy had a long history with God. She had been through many challenges and changes in her lifetime and God was always faithful to her. Because of her experience with God, Aunt Wealthy knew that God had a special plan for Millie. She said, "He is sending His very own Millie Keith, the bravest, most outspoken girl I know. There must be something very special He wants you to do in Pleasant Plains." Aunt Wealthy didn't have specific answers, but she knew enough about God to know that His plans were wonderfully adventuresome and trustworthy.

But Millie would have to discover this for herself. She would face many changes that would challenge her beliefs and emotions. Yet ultimately, those changes would help her discover God's goodness and trustworthiness.

Your Christian walk is a lifelong journey—a grand adventure—with many little adventures along the way that God allows in order to help you grow in trust and faith.

"Those are weeds!" The blur of tears in Millie's eyes made the weedy yard swim, looking almost like a garden. If she cried hard enough, this horrible thing might look a little like the home they had left with its large garden and endless flower beds. The June roses and the woodbine must be out by now—the air sweet with their delicious perfume— but they and those who had planted and tended them were far away from this desolate spot. How could she write to her friends that she was living in a warehouse?
— From *Millie's Unsettled Season*, page 111

One big challenge for Millie was their new home in Indiana. When Millie arrived in Pleasant Plains and took one look at what was to be their new home, it sent her emotions whirling.

Millie couldn't help thinking about her old home in Lansdale. She missed it so very much! Seeing her new home—a weedy, overgrown warehouse, filled her with longing for the beautiful home they had left behind. She was experiencing so many changes—and now the uncertainty of it all was starting to take a toll on her.

You might never move to the frontier, but one day you might have to move to a new state or change schools, churches, or jobs. Or your best friend might move away, changing everything for you and turning your world upside down, as Millie herself was experiencing.

Life is exciting, but it can be scary, too. It seems so unpredictable. Things could be going along fine and then something happens that creates sudden stress, confusion, and new challenges for you. "Growing up is never easy," said Aunt Wealthy to Millie in *Millie's Courageous Days*, (page 129).

Can you remember any situations in your life that seemed to turn your world upside down? Have you experienced a change in your life that was hard to handle? If so, describe it here.

How did this situation or change make you feel (scared, doubtful, worried, excited, etc.) and why?

How did you get through that situation?

Ecclesiastes 3:1 says, "There is a time for everything, and a *season* for every activity under heaven." This tells us that God designed things in life to change. Think about how the seasons of nature change. A tree sheds its leaves in the fall, begins to bloom again in the spring, and is in full bloom during summer; then the whole cycle begins again. Just as nature goes through different seasons, our own lives go through different seasons too.

 **Change is part of God's perfect design! Every "season" in life has a beginning and an end. So when an "unsettled" time comes, know that it will eventually turn into a more "settled" season. In the meantime, "unsettled seasons" are exciting opportunities to grow in your walk with God.**

How do you feel about change in general and why do you feel that way?

Look again at our memory verses so far, Proverbs 3:5–6 and John 14:1. Can you recite them by heart yet?

 **Change is not a bad thing; it is the natural plan of God. Though our circumstances or people in our lives will change, God will not. He is our rock to whom we can cling. He is faithful and reliable. He leads us even in the midst of our "unsettled seasons."**

Millie's circumstances changed drastically when she had to move to Pleasant Plains. But this experience, even though it was hard, gave Millie an opportunity to witness God's unchanging faithfulness in her life. God did not let her fall, as His Word promised!

 **Our response to change is very important. We need to embrace change and accept the different seasons that come and go in our lives. God is using them to stretch us and make us grow.**

Isaiah 64:8 says, "Yet, O L\ORD, you are our Father. We are the clay, you are the potter; we are all the work of your hand."

Would it be easy for a potter to work with stiff and hard clay? No, clay must be soft and pliable if it is to be worked with. A potter slowly mixes in water to make the clay soft enough to shape it into a useful vessel. When our hearts stubbornly resist the changes that God allows in our life, we are like stiff and hard clay in His hands. We will find ourselves fighting against the Potter's hands, when what He wants is to lovingly shape our lives for His purposes.

God is molding you into a vessel of His design. Entrust yourself to His skillful, all-knowing hands. Everything God makes is good.

Change can be thrust upon us unexpectedly or it can be by choice. In either case, change requires trust. Our memory verses tell us to "trust in the Lord with all your heart" (Proverbs 3:5) and "do not let your hearts be troubled" (John 14:1). When we give the Lord our heart, acknowledging and trusting Him with every circumstance in our lives, change (even difficult change) is easier to endure and accept.

Look up 2 Corinthians 3:18 and complete the missing words in the verse below:

And we, who with unveiled _____ all reflect the LORD'S _____, are

being _____ into his _____ with ever-increasing _____,

which comes from the LORD, who is the Spirit.

God is constantly working to mold and shape your heart so that you will reflect the love and character of Jesus. This is His highest aim! He will often allow changes to occur in your life so that if you yield to Him, your heart will be changed to be more like Jesus' heart.

Do you know that when you became a Christian, God did something fresh and new in your heart? He changed you! Second Corinthians 5:17 says, "Therefore, if anyone is in Christ, he is a new creation; the old has gone, the new has come!" Past and current changes in your life have been transforming you into the likeness of Jesus. This will continue throughout your life.

Since knowing Jesus, what are some of the old things that have gone, and what are the new things that have come? Write them in the space below.

Old Habits, Traits, Attitudes	New Habits, Traits, Attitudes

It is not always easy to trust God in the changes that come our way. We would rather trust our own ideas of how things should go. But as we will learn in chapter two, God is GOOD. God is LOVING. God is FAITHFUL. God is UNCHANGEABLE! We can TRUST HIM!

Although sometimes she had doubt and questions, Millie tried to trust God with all her heart during the difficult changes of her life. She learned to accept the changes and not fight against them. With her yielded heart, she was beginning to see that God had a good plan for her and her family, even when things were uncertain. Millie allowed the awkwardness and anxiety of change to help her grow into a stronger Christian.

Let Go & Let God

"Now, now, Millie dear," the older woman said, drawing her niece close. She stroked the hand she held. "There will be, perhaps, some adventures on the journey. I thought you yearned for adventure."

"I do! But I already know my adventure is completing my studies with Mr. Martin, and then Camilla and I will become the first female students to attend Tristan College. And then we're going to do something grand, something no woman has ever done before, something amazing! We will be doctors, or missionaries to some uncharted place on a faraway continent. We have it all planned! Aunty, I've been praying so hard about this, and I was sure God would find a way for me to stay in Lansdale. I don't want to leave my friends yet. Mamma even gave me a verse: 'Trust in the Lord with all your heart and lean not on your own understanding. In all your ways acknowledge him, and he will make your paths straight.'" She recited the words aloud, speaking earnestly as if she would carve the words into her heart. " 'He will make your paths straight.' Proverbs 3:6. I thought that meant if I trusted Him I could stay!"

Wealthy patted her hand in silence for a moment, then said, "You mustn't ignore verse 5, dear. 'Lean not on your own understanding.' "

—From *Millie's Unsettled Season*, page 5

In the above excerpt, we learn that Millie yearned for adventure in her life. But Millie had her "adventure" all planned out. She wanted to complete her studies and attend college. She had hopes of doing something grand and traveling to uncharted lands. Millie thought that if she trusted in God, if she "acknowledged" Him, she would get to stay in Lansdale. In other words, she thought that if she trusted God, that He would bless *her* plans. She thought she had her "straight path" all figured out.

In Proverbs 3:5–6, what do you think the phrase "lean not on your own understanding" means?

Why do you think the Bible tells us not to lean on our own understanding?

Leaning on your own understanding means you trust more in what *you think* than what *God thinks*. Whether you realize it or not, you are believing that you know more or know better than God.

Proverbs 20:24 says, "A man's steps are directed by the LORD. How then can anyone understand his own way?"

Isaiah 55:8–9 tells us that, "For my thoughts are not your thoughts, neither are your ways my ways," declares the LORD. "As the heavens are higher than the earth, so are my ways higher than your ways and my thoughts than your thoughts."

 **God's ways are OFTEN beyond our understanding. We must learn to trust Him instead of *our* understanding.**

Do you remember John 14:1, our memory verse for this chapter? Write it out here:

Millie had many plans and dreams in her heart—good plans that even involved serving God. Millie thought she knew what the future held for her. But in order to follow God, Millie had to let go of those plans. Remember what Aunt Wealthy taught Millie: Life is an _____!

The Bible says:

Do not boast about tomorrow, for you do not know what a day may bring forth. (Proverbs 27:1)

Many are the plans in a man's heart, but it is the LORD's purpose that prevails. (Proverbs 19:21)

 **The great "adventure" of life (and all the "little" adventures along the way) requires us to trust God. We must always be willing to let go of our own plans so He can fulfill His.**

Surrendering our plans to the Lord does not mean that they won't come to pass. It just means that we want God's plans even above our own. In Luke 22:42, we find that even Jesus had to choose to surrender His desires to His Father's will. "Father, if you are willing, take this cup from me; yet not my will, but yours be done."

Do *you* already have some plans (short-term or long-term) for your future? If so, summarize them here.

Would it be hard to let go of those plans? Why or why not?

Isaiah 43:18–19 says, "Forget the former things; do not dwell on the past. See, I am doing a new thing! Now it springs up; do you not perceive it? I am making a way in the desert and streams in the wasteland."

God calls us to "new things" all throughout our lifetime. Sometimes it's hard to let go of the "former things" in order to move on with God. Millie had to let go of the only home she had ever known. She had to leave behind her best friends, too. And although those things are hard to grapple with, God promises new beginnings and new opportunities.

He says, "I am making a way in the desert and streams in the wasteland"—a way which no one would have imagined possible! But that does not mean it will be easy.

The mood of the small group of family and friends gathered on Aunt Wealthy's vine-covered front porch on the last day of May was an odd mixture of excitement and tears. Millie was sure she knew exactly how the children of Israel had felt when they faced the Red Sea. She swallowed hard, and tried to smile at her friends.

"The girls do look sweet, Millie," said Bea as she adjusted the bow on Zillah's bonnet. Millie had to agree. Adah and Zillah were neat and clean in their new travel outfits. Millie had sewn Adah's herself, and Bea and Annabeth had finished Zillah's. "Do you suppose there will be shops in Pleasant Plains? I expect the fashions will be a bit backward—"

"Who cares about the fashions?" Camilla said. "What are you going to do about your studies? And are you taking books to read on the way?"

"I expect there will be shops," Millie said. "And I have packed my own books to read, though who knows how much time I will have, as I am minding the children." Millie bit her lip. Even if there were no shops, no parties, and not the slightest hint of fashion, she knew she could get by. But her friends! What would she do without them? Without Bea to help with dresses, without Annabeth to understand her heart before she even spoke, without Camilla to read sonnets?

"I wish I were taking you all with me!" Millie said. Annabeth took her hand and squeezed it.

—From *Millie's Unsettled Season*, page 51

 **Even though it might hurt, if we do not let go of someone or something when God is asking us to, we will cause ourselves even greater heartache and disappointment in the long run, and we will miss the adventure that God is leading us to go on.**

God is working in your life every day. There may be specific times when God asks you to let go of something big—like with Millie leaving her friends. But God also whispers little things in our ears too. For instance, God convicted Millie to be nicer to her brothers. She needed to let go of her impatience.

What "little" things might God be asking you to let go of? (For instance, anger toward your siblings, jealousy with your friends, disobedience toward your parents, etc.)

Ask God to search your heart and reveal anything He would want you to let go of in your life. List those things below. Pray that God will help you to let go of those things.

We do not know what is going to happen tomorrow. We do not know what "adventures" might come our way. Oh, we might have some good ideas, but we really cannot be sure. Only God knows the future, for only His plans are certain, and what is unknown to us is not unknown to Him. But as we grow in our trust of God, we will be ready and able to handle whatever challenges (adventures) come our way in the course of our everyday lives.

GOD IS TRUSTWORTHY! He is worthy of our trust! We will learn why in the next chapter.

Look back over this chapter. Ask the Holy Spirit to show you the most important things He wants you to remember. Put a star beside those truths and, in your own words, summarize below what He showed you.

Rewrite your thoughts as a prayer, asking God to help you grow and apply the truths He's taught you throughout the chapter.

Write out the memory verse for this chapter, John 14:1:

Write out the memory verse for our entire study, Proverbs 3:5–6:

CHAPTER

2

In God We Trust

In God We Trust

by heart

*F*or the LORD is good and his love endures forever; his faithfulness continues through all generations.   —PSALM 100:5

The Goodness of God

> *"I* don't follow Jesus because He can give me a life without pain. I follow Him because He is *good"* [explained Aunt Wealthy to Millie].
> —From *Millie's Courageous Days*, page 17

*N*ow we turn our attention to the most important subject of all—who God is. Just as you want people to know you for who you really are on the inside (your heart, your true character, etc.) God wants people to know Him for who He really is too. He has feelings and desires, emotions and thoughts. We can never begin to know everything about God, but He has given us enough glimpses of who He is in His Word and through His Son Jesus.

The more you *really* know God, the more you will trust in Him. Your greatest adventure in life will be your quest to know God. It's an adventure which will last your lifetime and on into eternity.

We see in the excerpt above that the goodness of God gave Aunt Wealthy the ability to follow Jesus through all the adventures of life—wherever He led her. This brings us to another key principle:

To trust God you must know that He is good ALL THE TIME and that EVERYTHING He does is good.

"You are good, and what you do is good," says Psalm 119:68.

Take some time to look deep into your heart. Do you believe that God is good all the time? Why or why not? Be honest with your response.

Read through the following verses. Think about what the verses are saying about God. Underline any key words that describe God's nature, character, or goodness.

Psalm 145:8–9
The LORD is gracious and compassionate, slow to anger and rich in love. The Lord is good to all; he has compassion on all he has made.

Psalm 145:17
The LORD is righteous in all his ways and loving toward all he has made.

Psalm 34:8
Taste and see that the LORD is good; blessed is the man who takes refuge in him.

Romans 8:28
And we know that in all things God works for the good of those who love him, who have been called according to his purpose.

Jeremiah 29:11
"For I know the plans I have for you," declares the LORD, "plans to prosper you and not to harm you, plans to give you hope and a future."

Deuteronomy 32:4
He is the Rock, his works are perfect, and all his ways are just. A faithful God who does no wrong, upright and just is he.

Re-read the verses again slowly and look back over the words you underlined. Then list all of the underlined words in the space below.

List any new things you learned about God from those verses.

From reading the above Scriptures, we can be assured that God is good to all and He is always good. Does knowing this about God help you want to trust Him more?

We must hold fast to these truths about God's nature when difficult seasons come. Bad things may happen, but know that you have a GOOD Heavenly Father controlling your life. In that knowledge lies the comfort and strength to continue on.

> *A* lifetime of adventure. That's what I want, thought Millie. But do I have enough faith to follow Jesus because He's good — no matter what happens?
>
> — From *Millie's Courageous Days*, page 32

Millie asked herself a hard question: "Do I have enough faith to follow Jesus because He's good—*no matter what happens?*" We need to be able to say with confidence, as David said during his trials, "I am still confident of this: I will see the goodness of the LORD in the land of the living" (Psalm 27:13).

In order for you to trust God, you need to know how much He loves you and be *absolutely convinced* of His goodness. This doesn't happen overnight. Knowing God is a lifelong journey. Each day we can learn something new about God's goodness and love for us, and each day our faith and trust in Him can grow stronger.

Write out our memory verse for this chapter, Psalm 100:5, here:

As you begin to learn more about God's *everlasting* goodness and faithfulness, you will be able to trust God more and more—no matter what life throws your way!

"Surely goodness and love will follow me all the days of my life," said David in Psalm 23:6.

The Faithfulness of God

"$\mathcal{M}$amma?"

Marcia looked up with a smile. "Yes, Millie?" ….

"How do you learn to trust the Lord?"

Marcia wiped her wet, soapy arms on her apron, then walked over to the table and pulled out a chair. "Sit down, Millie," she said.

Millie sat in the chair.

"Now, daughter, what is keeping you from tumbling to the floor?"

Millie looked surprised. "The chair!"

"Aren't you afraid it will let you fall?"

"Of course not. It's never let me fall before."

Marcia went back to the washtub. "I can trust in God because He has never let me fall. But everyone has a first time for trusting Him. Everyone has to learn for themselves that He loves them and won't let them fall. This is a good time to learn, my love."

— From *Millie's Unsettled Season*, pages 15–16

Millie had to learn for herself that God was trustworthy and faithful. Just like Millie, you must discover for yourself that God is faithful to you.

The book of Psalms provides great insight about God's faithfulness. For example, Psalm 37:23–24 says, "If the LORD delights in a man's way, he makes his steps firm; though he stumble, he will not fall, for the LORD upholds him with his hand."

As with many of God's promises, there is a requirement or condition in order for us to receive this promise. What is it?

What do you think that requirement or condition means for you in your life?

Psalm 55:22 says, "Cast your cares on the LORD and he will sustain you; he will never let the righteous fall." According to that verse, what is God's promise to you?

What is the one step you are required to take as a condition of the promise in Psalm 55:22?

Look up Psalm 9:10 and complete the missing words below:

Those who _____ your _____ will _____ in you, for you, LORD, have

_____ _____ those who _____ you.

Have you ever felt *forsaken*? Or in other words, have you ever felt ignored, left out, lonely, or isolated? Briefly describe your experience.

People may let us down, but Psalm 9:10 promises us that God will never forsake those who love and seek Him. When you face times of difficulty or uncomfortable changes, recognize that it is an opportunity to trust God and His faithfulness to you. Call on Him. He won't ignore your call for help!

In the excerpt at the beginning of this lesson, Millie's mother told her that everyone has a first time for trusting God. She said, "Everyone has to learn for themselves that He loves them and won't let them fall. This is a good time to learn, my love."

But in the following passage, we see that Millie's mother had to continually trust in the faithfulness of God. She was believing that the same God who was faithful to her in the past (in Lansdale, Ohio) would be just as faithful in the unknown future (in Pleasant Plains, Indiana).

"It was a beautiful home," her mother whispered. "God blessed me with eight children there. And the same God that blessed me there will be with us wherever He leads us." Millie and her mother turned back together, just as four prancing steeds swept around the corner, and swaying and rolling, the coach dashed up to the gate.

—From *Millie's Unsettled Season*, page 52

 **It is good to regularly pause and remember the many ways God has been faithful to you in the past. Like statues erected to commemorate a significant event, these memories will remind you of God's faithfulness and prepare you for the challenges before you.**

Altars were often built by the Israelites to remind them of God's faithfulness. (See Genesis 12:7) Typically made of stones, altars were a tangible way to "record" a special time or experience in their walk of faith.

Like the altars of the past, journaling can be very helpful in capturing the special, faith-inspiring moments and memories that will occur throughout your personal walk of faith. (*Millie's Daily Diary* is a journal uniquely designed for that purpose.) If you haven't done journaling before, try your hand at it now and write in the space below a time in your past when God led you to success or triumph in a time of personal trial.

We learned earlier that life will bring seasons of change in which everything around us will seem to be in a state of fluctuation.

We must know that in the midst of our changing world, God is the one constant, steady force. God is our Rock.

What characteristics or qualities does the image of a rock bring to your mind?

Have you ever stood on a rock jetty with the turbulent pounding of the ocean surf surrounding you? If your feet are not planted firmly on that rock jetty, you'll be swept away. God is that solid, steady, immovable place. Planting your feet firmly on Him means you are choosing to trust Him with all your heart. Then when the storms of life come, you will not be swept away.

Here are some verses that show that God does not change. Circle the words in italics:

<u>Hebrews 13:8</u>
Jesus Christ *is the same* yesterday and today and forever.

<u>James 1:17</u>
Every good and perfect gift is from above, coming down from the Father of the heavenly lights, who *does not change* like shifting shadows.

<u>Psalm 62:7</u>
My salvation and my honor depend on God; he is my mighty *rock*, my *refuge*.

Here are some more verses. Look each one up in your Bible and complete the missing words below. Explain in your own words what it teaches you about God's faithfulness.

<u>Romans 8:38–39</u>

For I am _____ that neither death nor _____, neither _____ nor demons, neither the present nor the _____, nor any _____, neither _____ nor depth, nor anything else in ____ creation, will be able to separate us from the _____ of God that is in Christ Jesus our LORD.

Psalm 145:13

Your kingdom is an _____ kingdom, and your dominion
_____ through all generations. The LORD is _____
to all his _____ and loving toward all he has made.

2 Thessalonians 3:3

But the LORD is _____, and he will _____ and
protect you from the evil one.

1 John 1:9

If we _____ our sins, he is _____ and just and will
_____ us our sins and _____ us from all unrighteousness.

Write out this chapter's memory verse, Psalm 100:5, in the space below.

God's faithfulness continues through *all* generations! That is a very long time! Turn
in your Bible to Luke 3:23–38 and read the passage. Count how many generations there
were from Adam to Jesus and fill in the number here: _____. It would be difficult
to count the number of generations from Jesus to you, but you can be assured that God's
faithfulness has endured to *your* generation!

No wonder David says in Psalm 89:1, "I will sing of the LORD's great love forever;
with my mouth I will make your faithfulness known through all generations."

The Help of God

"When God has a plan, He makes a way." In the following excerpt, God made a way
by finding a buyer for the Keith's house in Lansdale. It needed to be sold before they
could move to Pleasant Plains. God had a plan for the Keiths and He helped them achieve
His plan. They only needed to trust Him.

"Pappa just sent word. Mr. Garlin's nephew is willing to buy our house! But we have to be out by the first of June—in just two more weeks!"

Millie looked at the pile of fabric waiting to be turned into dresses, pants, and shirts. "Couldn't God have taken a little longer, Mamma? How can we possibly finish in time?"

"When you ask God for help, sometimes you get a surprise," Aunt Wealthy said. "Just think about the children of Israel, when they left Egypt. The Red Sea before them and Pharaoh's army behind them. When they cried out for God to save them, I'm sure they didn't expect Him to tell them to march right through the sea! When God has a plan, He makes a way!" She stood and gestured, as if by a wave of her hand she would part the calico and chintz and they would sort themselves into neatly sewn garments.

—From *Millie's Unsettled Season*, pages 37–38

List some ways God has helped your family achieve a goal or overcome a hardship. If you're uncertain, ask your mother or father to help you remember times when God helped your family.

At first Millie didn't see that God was actually helping her family by providing a buyer for their house. In her heart she wished to stay in Pleasant Plains for a little bit longer. It was hard for her to imagine leaving her friends, and besides that, there was lots of work to be done before they could move! But Aunt Wealthy reminded Millie that when we ask God for help, we sometimes get a surprise! Certainly the Israelites never expected God to part the Red Sea for them! But they trusted that God would not let them drown in the waters—they trusted God's help!

When we ask God for help, we must be willing to let God work in our lives however He sees fit, even when God does things that are different from how we expected.

This is another great reason for trusting God: He knows the best way to help us and we have to trust His judgment!

Second Samuel 22:31–34 says, "As for God, his way is perfect; the word of the LORD is flawless. He is a shield for all who take refuge in him. For who is God besides the LORD? And who is the Rock except our God? It is God who arms me with strength and makes my way perfect. He makes my feet like the feet of a deer; he enables me to stand on the heights."

According to this verse, how does God provide help?

In this verse, the word "heights" can represent the challenges in our lives. God can make us like a sure-footed deer that can scale the rocky precipices without slipping.

In what areas of your life do you need God's help right now? Are there things you are fearful of?

Take a few minutes right now to pray and ask God to help you in those areas. Then believe that He *will* send help.

God is always watching over you to help you. One way you can trust God's help is to know the promises He makes to you through the Scriptures.

Millie turned to her Bible and searched out God's promises. This helped her to trust that God would be there for her.

The following verses are God speaking directly to you. Under each verse, summarize in your own words the specific ways God promises to help you. Ask the Holy Spirit to open the eyes of your heart to these truths.

Isaiah 41:10 — So do not fear, for I am with you; do not be dismayed, for I am your God. I will strengthen you and help you; I will uphold you with my righteous right hand.

Psalm 32:8 — I will instruct you and teach you in the way you should go; I will counsel you and watch over you.

Joshua 1:9 — Have I not commanded you? Be strong and courageous. Do not be terrified; do not be discouraged, for the LORD your God will be with you wherever you go.

We grow in faith and trust by reading God's Word. The more you learn about God's promises to help you, the more courageous you will become! You will be able to enjoy all the grand adventures God has for your life without shrinking away in fear.

Hold tightly to God's helping hand even though it may come in an unexpected way. He will lead you along the unfamiliar paths.

Write down some examples of surprising or unusual ways God helped people in the Bible. We will give you some names to get you started, but add others to the list.

People God Helped	The Way God Helped Them
Daniel and the lion's den	
Peter's escape from prison	
The Israelites crossing the Red Sea	
Joshua and the walls of Jericho	

God is creative and mysterious! Imagine what Daniel must have felt when he was in the lion's den! What did Peter think when the angel came to him in prison and rescued him? These men and women lived for God—and their lives were full of adventure. They had to trust God with their very lives—and God's help never failed them!

Sometimes, such as in these cases, God chooses to help us as we go *through* the trial. Daniel had to go *into* the lion's den, Peter was thrown *in* prison, the Israelites had to pass *through* the Red Sea, and Joshua had to *march around* the city seven times, though it looked foolish. God does not always spare us from the affliction, although He may choose to at times. But His promise of help is that He will lead you through.

 **Trust God that He *will* help you, and trust His perfect plan for *how* He sends you help!**

You are no different from Daniel or Peter! God used them in miraculous ways because they trusted Him. Imagine what God will do in your life as you learn to trust Him more and more!

Psalm 28:7 proclaims, "The LORD is my strength and my shield; my heart trusts in him, and I am helped."

The Sovereignty of God

"The Bible all happened so long ago," Helen finished. The rest of the class looked relieved that someone had said it, and it hadn't been them.

Millie waited. She had seen that twinkle in Aunt Wealthy's eye before.

"It did happen long ago," Aunt Wealthy agreed. "But it happened to people just like you. Did you ever think of that? And most of the stories that were written down were the big, important battles. But don't you think God cared about Joshua on the days when he wasn't marching around Jericho?"

"Well, I suppose He did," Bill ventured. "Doesn't the Bible say God loves us?"

" 'For God so loved the world that He gave His one and only Son,' " Wealthy quoted. "And if you love someone, do you care what happens to them only on certain days?"

"No," said Celestia Ann. "You care every day, and night, too. Jes' like it says in Psalm 23, 'The Lord is my shepherd'… He is always watching out for you!"

"I'll tell you a secret," Wealthy said, lowering her voice. "God cares about the Christmas social. He cares about fun."

— From *Millie's Unsettled Season*, pages 211–212

God is sovereign. This means that He rules and reigns throughout the universe. He is all-knowing and all-powerful. He possesses supreme power over all the earth. It means that God has control over the affairs of nature and history. Nothing happens without God's knowledge of it. He is our Ruler, and there is no other force in the universe that is greater than He is!

To better understand the concept of God's sovereignty over the universe, let's examine some more Scripture verses.

Proverbs 15:3 says, "The eyes of the LORD are everywhere, keeping watch on the wicked and the good." God not only watches the activities of Christians, He also watches those who don't serve Him! No one is exempt from God's view. God is aware of it all! How is this an example of God's sovereignty? Write your answer in the space below.

Since God is in control, He can do whatever He wants with His unlimited power and wisdom. Daniel 4:35 tells us, "He does as he pleases with the powers of heaven and the peoples of the earth. No one can hold back his hand or say to him: 'What have you done?'" When we begin to see that everything is God's, we can have a peace that God can do what He wants with His creation.

We know from history that rulers and kings can be conquered, kingdoms and governments fall, and cities can be destroyed and rebuilt again. But in God's Kingdom, this is not so. Daniel 6:26 proclaims, "For he is the living God and he endures forever; his kingdom will not be destroyed, his dominion will never end."

 **Knowing that God is in control of the earth and that His dominion will never end should give you incredible peace.**

Slowly reread each verse in this lesson so far. What do these verses tell you about God and His supreme power (sovereignty) in the earth?

 **Even though God tends to the matters of the universe, He is sovereign in *your* life as well.**

Do you trust that God governs and cares about *all* the details of your life? If not, what are some of them that you struggle with?

Read through Psalm 139:1–16 below. This passage of Scripture also reveals something about the sovereignty of God, but these verses have a more personal touch. They assure us that God has had His hands on *our* lives since before we were even born!

O LORD, you have searched me and you know me. You know when I sit and when I rise; you perceive my thoughts from afar. You discern my going out and my lying down; you are familiar with all my ways. Before a word is on my tongue you know it completely, O LORD. You hem me in—behind and before; you have laid your hand upon me. Such knowledge is too wonderful for me, too lofty for me to attain. Where can I go from your Spirit? Where can I flee from your presence? If I go up to the heavens, you are there; if I make my bed in the depths, you are there. If I rise on the wings of the dawn, if I settle on the far side of the sea, even there your hand will guide me, your right hand will hold me fast. If I say, "Surely the darkness will hide me and the light become night around me," even the darkness will not be dark to you; the night will shine like the day, for darkness is as light to you. For you created my inmost being; you knit me together in my mother's womb. I praise you because I am fearfully and wonderfully made; your works are wonderful, I know that full well. My frame was not hidden from you when I was made in the secret place. When I was woven together in the depths of the earth, your eyes saw my unformed body. All the days ordained for me were written in your book before one of them came to be.

Now go back over the passage and underline in one color of ink every word or phrase that speaks of God's knowledge of you. Look for different words that mean the same as "know," such as "discern" and "perceive." Next, with a second color of ink, circle all the words or phrases that speak of His loving care toward us (hint: look for references about how He works in our lives with His hands, such as the word "knitting" suggests).

Do you see from this passage how intimately God cares for you? Picture God tenderly and lovingly knitting your life together, just as a mother-to-be would joyfully knit a blanket for her unborn child.

Take some time now to pray Psalm 139:1–16 out loud to God. Praying Scripture back to God is a wonderful way to communicate with Him, and these verses both acknowledge God's power and give Him praise.

Do you realize how special you really are to God? He has His loving eyes on you—all the time! He knows you inside and out, and He knows the plans He has for your life. Even in this big, complicated world, God wants you to rest in His sovereignty (His supreme power) and know that you are safe and secure.

Millie's mother and father felt sure that God would provide and care for them in Pleasant Plains. They trusted in God's sovereignty. They felt secure, even in the midst of great change in their family's circumstances. Why? Because they knew God. They knew His character and His promises. They held fast to Him through their personal relationship with Him and through their study of His Word. These are the same things you need to do.

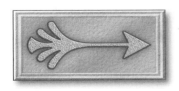 **You will feel more secure in your life if you trust God's sovereignty.**

In your own words, describe what God's sovereignty means to your life. If that is difficult to do, review this lesson, paying special attention to the Scripture verses. Pray and ask the Lord to help you understand the meaning of His sovereignty to you.

Sometimes it's hard to trust that God is in control of our lives, especially when we face tough times. Millie struggled with trusting God's sovereignty in her life. She wasn't so sure that God was making the best decision for her when it was decided that they were going to move to Pleasant Plains. In the midst of her own doubts, Millie clung to one of her favorite Bible verses, Proverbs 3:5–6, our main Bible verse for this study. From memory, complete the missing words in the verse below.

_____ in the LORD with all your _____ and lean not on your own _____;

in all your ways _____ him, and he will make your paths straight.

From memory, can you complete the missing words in Psalm 100:5, too?

For the LORD is _____ and his _____ endures _____; his _____

continues through _____ generations.

Even though Millie had doubts and questions, she was determined to continue on in her pursuit of God. She never gave up! Millie wrestled with God's Word and she sought advice from people she trusted, like her mother and Aunt Wealthy.

You can be assured that God is sovereign in *your* life! You might have some questions or doubts like Millie did, but if you press into the Word and share your struggle with those you trust, God will lead you and reveal Himself to you! You will be able to face the uncertainties and changes in life with confidence, because you will be able to say, "God is in control!"

The Plans of God

"*A*re you getting done fast, Mamma?" Zillah asked. "Can we sleep in the Big Yellow House tonight?"

"Not tonight. We've scrubbed the wood floors and I want them to dry thoroughly before we move in. We will go back to the Union for our supper and to sleep tonight. But tomorrow…"

"We will be in our own house!" Fan yelled.

"Not the nice house we used to have, though," sighed Zillah.

"What!" Marcia said. "You are not telling me you don't like our new home! Did Indians ever visit at our old house? Just think of it! They were the first of our new neighbors to greet us! And we had no buffalo robes, or houses made of saplings to play in. It is not the same, but I am sure God has a very good plan for the Keiths!"

—From *Millie's Unsettled Season*, pages 135–136

Marcia Keith trusted in God's sovereignty and goodness for their lives. We know that because she said, "I am *sure* God has a *very good* plan for the Keiths!"

 **When you allow God to be sovereign over your life, you must trust in His plans, even if they are not what you expected! You must trust that His plans are good.**

Do you trust that God has a "very good plan" for your life? Why or why not?

Millie was unsure about God's plans for her. Moving to Pleasant Plains was certainly something she never expected. It seemed that she was headed into the great "unknown." There were many questions, doubts, and fears that Millie had to sort out.

As we read in Psalm 139, God is intimately aware of all your ways and has a well-laid plan for your life. God's plans are good. He wants to be a tender, loving, Good Shepherd, and lead you through the unfamiliar places. He is always with you.

Search out the following verses in your Bible and fill in the blanks:

Proverbs 16:9

In his heart a man _____, but the

LORD _____.

Proverbs 20:24

A man's _____ are _____ by the LORD. How then

can anyone _____ his _____ way?

Jeremiah 10:23

I know, O LORD, that a man's _____ is _____ his own; it is _____ for man to _____ his steps.

Jeremiah 29:11

"For I know the _____ I have for you," declares the LORD, "_____ to _____ you and not to harm you, _____ to give you _____ and a _____."

Out of these four verses, which one are you drawn to the most? Why?

After reading these Scriptures, how do you now feel about God's plans for your life?

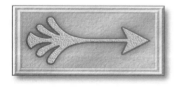

God has special plans for you. Right now you may not see all of the details or know all of the answers, but as you walk with God on a daily basis, His plans will unfold before you.

Psalm 138:8 — The LORD will fulfill his purpose for me.

Philippians 1:6 — Being confident of this, that he who began a good work in you will carry it on to completion until the day of Christ Jesus.

As we seek to obey and follow God in all our ways, He will see to it that His plans are fulfilled in our lives. HE will do it; it is not our responsibility to make it happen. We just need to be faithful and trust Him along the way.

When you think about God's plans, you don't have to know the "big picture" of your entire life. God has a new plan for you every day.

There may be short-term plans God will reveal, like saving up for a youth missions trip. Or perhaps God will lay a plan of prayer on your heart, where you get into the habit of daily, consistent prayer. Maybe God wants you to plan a specific time each week for Bible study. God has great purpose—even in the small plans.

What are some "small" plans *God* might have for you? (Such as completing a Bible study, reading a certain book of the Bible, joining a prayer group, getting along with your brothers and sisters, etc.)

Are there any long-term plans that you sense *God* may be drawing you toward? If so, describe them here.

What you accomplish today matters for tomorrow! Your obedience to God's plans now (like developing a consistent prayer time each day) establishes a foundation for the things God has for you in the future.

Millie knew that God wanted her to learn to be patient with her younger brothers—it was a short-term plan that God had for her. Millie obeyed (even though it was hard!) and began to lean on the guidance of the Holy Spirit to help her. It took some time, but Millie began to see changes in her behavior towards her brothers. Maybe her obedience to God's prompting built a foundation for her to be patient toward Miss Drybread later on in Pleasant Plains! If Millie had not obeyed God's plan to be patient with her brothers, perhaps it would have been much harder for her to deal with Damaris Drybread.

Can you think of a time when God asked you to do something little, which then helped prepare you for something bigger?

Look back over this chapter. Ask the Holy Spirit to show you the most important things He wants you to remember. Put a star beside those truths and, in your own words, summarize below what He showed you.

Rewrite your thoughts as a prayer, asking God to help you grow and apply the truths He's taught you throughout the chapter.

Write out the memory verse for this chapter, Psalm 100:5:

Write out the memory verse for our entire study, Proverbs 3:5–6:

CHAPTER

Pioneering with God

Lesson 1
A New Mindset

Lesson 2
New Opportunities

Lesson 3
Why Me?

Lesson 4
Godly Role Models

Lesson 5
Courage for the Adventure

Pioneering with God

*F*or we are God's workmanship, created in Christ Jesus to do good works, which God prepared in advance for us to do.

— EPHESIANS 2:10

A New Mindset

*M*illie looked at her aunt's peaceful face, which was upturned toward the sun. How hard it must be for her to live in a house full of children, with curtains for walls. Sound carried right through the fabric, and from the moment the Keiths had set foot in the warehouse, the only quiet times had been when the children were in bed asleep....

On their journey to Pleasant Plains they had spent some weeks aboard a canal packet, sharing one cabin with all the passengers and crew. It was very hard to never be alone. The Big Yellow House was just the same, Millie realized. Because of the constant noise, one never had the sense of being alone.

"How do you manage?" Millie asked. "You were used to having your own house . . . now to be part of such a large crowd, in a house with fabric walls."

"A large, noisy crowd!" Aunt Wealthy laughed. "But it's not so bad, really. The children of Israel lived in tents for forty years, remember? They had to listen to each other, and to their neighbors as well."

— From *Millie's Courageous Days*, pages 58–59

*A*t this point in our study, we have seen how Millie was learning that life is an adventure in which we must trust in God. When Millie's parents announced that they were moving to Pleasant Plains whether she wanted to or not, she began her own adventure in trusting God.

In chapter one we learned *what* it means to trust in God. Our emphasis was on *trust*. In chapter two we looked at *who* God is and *why* He is trustworthy. We learned that it's vital to know God personally and understand His nature and character — especially His goodness and faithfulness, which are unchangeable. Otherwise, it's hard to trust. After all, we don't typically trust strangers. We need to *know* God before we can fully trust Him.

Now it is time to turn our attention to the subject of *how* we walk in trust. How do we lean on God day by day, let alone during grand adventures like the one Millie was about to experience? In this chapter we will begin our journey of learning the *how* part of trusting God.

Let's go back to our memory verse for this study, Proverbs 3:5–6, and take a closer look at verse 5. Finish the verse:

Trust in the LORD with all your heart and _____ on your own

_____.

In chapter one we talked about what it means to "lean not on your own understanding." We discovered that leaning on your own understanding means you are trusting more in what *you think* than what *God thinks*.

Can you think of a time when you trusted in your own understanding of a situation and got it wrong?

For example, when God asked Moses to go back to Egypt and free the people from Pharaoh, Moses initially thought that he couldn't possibly do what God asked him. Moses viewed the situation from his own understanding of himself. He saw himself as weak and slow of speech. He was convinced that he was not the right choice for the job. But God knew differently and Moses had to trust God's judgment and lean on God's understanding—not his own.

If we are to trust God, early on we must deal with an important element—our minds! We need to have a new way of thinking—*God's* way of thinking. We must learn to think like He thinks. We need a new mindset.

According to the dictionary, a mindset is "a fixed mental attitude or disposition that predetermines a person's responses to and interpretations of situations." In other words, your mindset is how you think about things or how you view life, situations, yourself, others, and the world. It is your *viewpoint*. A "viewpoint" is a position from which something is observed or considered; a mental view or outlook on a particular situation; a point of view.

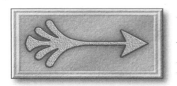 **We each have a unique viewpoint in life, but first and foremost we need to align our thoughts and beliefs with God's viewpoint.**

In the excerpt at the beginning of this lesson, Millie was considering Aunt Wealthy's peaceful face. Look back at the passage and then in the chart below consider the difference between how Millie probably felt and how Aunt Wealthy felt.

Circumstance	Millie's Viewpoint	Aunt Wealthy's Viewpoint
constant noise	annoying	not as bad as the Israelites had to bear
large crowd	hard to never be alone	not as bad as the Israelites had to bear
not her own house	frustrating	not as bad as the Israelites had to bear
paper walls	far from ideal	not as bad as the Israelites had to bear

What differences do you see in their viewpoints?

Whose perspective is more Christlike, and why?

What are the benefits of having a more Christlike viewpoint?

The Bible tells us in Romans 12:2, "Do not conform any longer to the pattern of this world, but be transformed by the renewing of your mind. Then you will be able to test and approve what God's will is—his good, pleasing and perfect will."

To renew your mind means to adopt the thoughts of Christ. A Christlike viewpoint is the mindset you must adopt for your life. This is pleasing to God and allows you to know and do God's good, pleasing, and perfect will in every adventure you face.

"How can I have Christ's viewpoint?" you might ask. Look up 1 Corinthians 2:11–16 in your Bible and read through the passage. You will see that it ends with a startling statement. It tells us that "we have the mind of Christ." This means that we have the ability, through the power of God's Holy Spirit that lives inside of us, to think the thoughts of Christ and see things from His viewpoint.

Philippians 4:19 says, "And my God will meet all your needs according to his glorious riches in Christ Jesus." Look back at the chart on the previous page. Can you see that Aunt Wealthy believed that God would meet all her needs?

Can you see an attitude of gratitude in Aunt Wealthy's comments as well? Explain.

You can be sure that Aunt Wealthy was not blind to the unpleasantries of their journey to Pleasant Plains and their new home and circumstances once they got there. She saw the very same things that everyone else did.

But why was her viewpoint different? Because she had the mind of Christ! Over the years, she had learned to see things not just from a natural perspective (the things you see with your physical eyes) but also from a spiritual perspective (the things you see with spiritual eyes). She had trained herself to see things from *God's* viewpoint! No wonder her thoughts were filled with faith and gratitude. She had a godly mindset—a right way of thinking.

Second Corinthians 10:5 says, "We demolish arguments and every pretension that sets itself up against the knowledge of God, and we take captive every thought to make it obedient to Christ." Aunt Wealthy knew what to do with her thoughts—she took them captive to make them obedient to Christ!

New Opportunities

> "*H*ello, Aunt Wealthy. Have you heard the news?" [asked Stuart Keith].
>
> "That you are going to Indiana, Stuart? Yes, I've heard something about it," Wealthy said with a twinkle in her eye. "Not content to live in this civilized and cultured town, are you?"
>
> "Lawyers are not so plentiful there, and as more folks move in, legal services will be in great demand. I plan to open my own practice. And land is cheap. I'll invest in a portion of it and hope to see it increase in value as the town grows. However," his voice grew solemn, "it will mean the sundering of some very dear ties here."
>
> —From *Millie's Unsettled Season*, pages 21–22

Moving to Pleasant Plains meant *opportunity* for the Keith family. Since there weren't many lawyers in the growing town, Stuart saw an opportunity to grow his own business. And since land was plentiful, the Keith family would be able to purchase land and watch the value of the land grow with time. Stuart Keith was a Christian. He prayed about the decision and felt that God was leading them.

Like Mr. Keith, the pioneers of the 1800s looked to the West and saw *opportunity*. And in truth, there were lots of new opportunities for the people who moved West. If those people didn't get excited about the new opportunities, they would never have traveled

West and expanded the borders of the United States. Our country would not be the same as it is today.

Every member of the Keith family had to trust that God, in His sovereignty, was directing their lives—on purpose. They had to trust that good opportunities and wonderful adventures awaited them in their new hometown. They had to see with eyes of faith and look to God to give them courage. The Keith family had to adopt a new mindset—the kind of faith-filled, Christlike mindset that we learned about in the last lesson. We could call this a "pioneer mindset."

> *We will be a part of something grand—building a town!* [thought Millie].
> —From *Millie's Unsettled Season*, page 40
>
> "*We will be pioneers ourselves,*" responded Stuart.
> —From *Millie's Unsettled Season*, page 115

What comes to mind when you hear the word *pioneer*?

Let's look at the definition of the word *pioneer*.

> Pioneer—a person who is among those who first enter or settle a region, thus opening it for occupation and development by others; one of a group of foot soldiers detailed to make roads, dig entrenchments, etc., in advance of the main body; to take part in the beginnings of; a person or group that originates or helps open up a new line of thought or activity; one who establishes a new method or technical development.

Pioneers are not just people from the past who moved out to undeveloped territories in the early years of our country. We have pioneers today. A modern pioneer might be someone who develops a new computer technology, makes a medical breakthrough, initiates some kind of social reform, or develops a new style of music. These pioneers have a large, visible impact on our culture, but it is important to understand that people who make smaller, less visible contributions are pioneers too. For example, a mother who comes up with a new strategy to help her child learn to read and a student who develops a fundraising idea for her volleyball team are both pioneers. They are pioneers who are impacting their world in their own creative ways.

Do you want to be a pioneer? Would you like to be a pioneer for God? No, you don't have to pack up your belongings and move out West on a wagon. Pioneering for God means following God every day, watching for doors of opportunity He opens for you, and going wherever He leads you. You can be a pioneer at school, at a friend's house, at home, or at the store. You can pack up the world's opinions and demands and take on the attitude and call of Christ for your life instead!

God wants you to be a pioneer for Him—someone through whom He can shine His light into the world in creative ways. He wants to use you to blaze new trails for His Kingdom!

Isaiah 54:2 says, "Enlarge the place of your tent, stretch your tent curtains wide, do not hold back; lengthen your cords, strengthen your stakes. For you will spread out to the right and to the left...."

As pioneers we must be prepared to be stretched by God. He wants to expand our hearts and our influence for Him in the world.

Like any good shepherd, Jesus wants to lead His sheep to greener pastures (Psalm 23:2). After a period of grazing in one spot, the sheep will have consumed the supply of rich, green grass. The shepherd knows it is vital for the sheep's health to lead them on to fresh meadows, but often the comfortable sheep are quite reluctant to leave. Remember, God will lead us on paths of life. To stay means stagnation and starvation. To move on means ever-increasing nourishment and life.

Pioneers for God (spiritual pioneers) are not just interested in going somewhere physically (like to a new city or state), but want to go to "new places" in their walk with the Lord. They are willing to renew their minds with the Word of God so that they can think the thoughts of Christ, and are willing to be "sent out" to reach the lost. These things require the kind of courage and trust in God that we learned about in chapter one.

The Keiths saw opportunity in Pleasant Plains, so they stepped out boldly in faith and courage. Likewise, God brings us opportunities every day—opportunities to grow in our walk with God. For instance, you can be a pioneer for God by simply showing kindness to someone in your neighborhood or at church or obeying your parents. It means learning to hear God and doing as He asks.

For example, you might have a teammate on your sports team who is struggling. Instead of making fun of her, you feel like God is asking you to help her. So you stay after practice for a few minutes to help her run through the drill a few more times. By trusting God and being obedient to Him by showing kindness to your teammate, you are actually pioneering in God's Kingdom! This may seem like a small thing, but we need to try to see the "bigger picture" in God's plan!

 **Our little acts of trusting God today are very important in making history tomorrow!**

Maybe because of your help, your struggling teammate is encouraged, and instead of giving up the sport because she was failing, she tries even harder. Suppose that years later she becomes an Olympic athlete! Your kind words and gestures can change the course of a person's life! Now that's making history for God!

Abraham was one of God's pioneers in the Old Testament. God said to Abraham, "Leave your country, your people and your father's household and go to the land I will show you" (Genesis 12:1). God invited Abraham on a grand adventure. Abraham had to trust God, just like the Keiths did!

Did you know that Abraham's act of trusting God—leaving his country and going into a land that God would show him—set in motion a whole series of events that changed history? Because Abraham obeyed God, God fulfilled His promise and Abraham became the father of many nations—nations that are still growing and thriving to this very day! It's not so hard to be a history maker or a pioneer for God. We just need to hear God and follow Him faithfully on the great adventure! Abraham was part of a big picture in God's plans, and as a child of God, you share in the same destiny!

 **Pioneering for God involves us in the "big picture" of God's plans. We cannot see the big picture, but He can.**

God is always calling His people into new things so they will learn to trust in Him. The Bible is full of examples. We have listed a few to get you started. See if you can think of any other people in the Bible that God called into such new things that they had to trust Him in a major way.

People in the Bible who had to *Really* Trust God

Person	New Thing They Were Called To	Their Lesson in Trust
Noah	God instructing Noah to build the ark	
Moses	God sending Moses to talk to Pharaoh	
The Israelites	The Israelites leaving Egypt for the Promised Land	

Pioneering for God involves recognizing divinely orchestrated opportunities and moving forward in faith and trust. As God's pioneers, we need to watch for new opportunities that God brings our way and then be faithful and obedient to pursue them.

As we learned earlier, in Isaiah 43:18–19, God said, "Forget the former things; do not dwell on the past. See, I am doing a new thing! Now it springs up; do you not perceive it? I am making a way in the desert and streams in the wasteland."

When we trust in God, He gives us the ability to do the things HE wants us to do. We might have to walk through our adventures by faith and not by sight, but God makes a way even when there is none. God made a way for the Keiths to make the move from Ohio to Pleasant Plains; He provided a buyer for their house in Lansdale. He did a new thing in their lives. Likewise, God will make a way for you in the good works He has prepared for you! First Thessalonians 5:24 says, "The One who calls you is faithful and he will do it."

Do you ever wish God would send you a map of your life so that you could see your future all planned out? But He doesn't work that way, does He? He wants us to have faith and trust in Him day by day. But we can take comfort from Psalm 25:12, which says, "Who, then, is the man that fears the LORD? He will instruct him in the way chosen for him." God will instruct you in the way He has chosen for you. Each new situation God brings you is somehow a piece of a giant puzzle. How great that we get to be used by God in such grand ways!

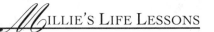

Think about your interests, passions, and skills. Using your imagination, what are some ways God might use you to be a modern-day pioneer?

Interests, Passions, Skills	Being a "Pioneer for God"

In your own words, finish the sentence: As a modern-day pioneer I must have a new mindset, which means_____

_____

_____

_____

Why Me?

*M*illie stood for a moment and watched as her aunt, armed with a large cotton umbrella, marched briskly towards the business part of town. Could Aunt Wealthy be right? Did Jesus have something for her, Mildred Eleanor Keith, to do in Pleasant Plains? What possible difference could a twelve-year-old make in a frontier town?
— From *Millie's Unsettled Season*, pages 10–11

Ephesians 2:10 is our memory verse for this chapter. Complete the missing words in the verse below.

We are God's _____, created in Christ Jesus to do _____ works,

which God prepared in _____ for us to do.

God has prepared good works for you to accomplish in your lifetime!

How does it make you feel knowing that God has good works planned for you?

The word *workmanship* in this verse also means "a work of art." Do you see yourself as God's workmanship or a "work of art"? Why or why not?

God has plans for your life—plans and purposes that are abundantly above anything you can imagine. You are a *priceless* work of art created to achieve good works throughout your lifetime. God's plans for you are part of a really big picture that you cannot see.

"Now to him who is able to do *immeasurably more* than all we ask or imagine, according to his power that is at work within us, to him be glory in the church and in Christ Jesus throughout all generations, for ever and ever! Amen." (Ephesians 3:20–21)

Have you ever wondered if God could really use you—what difference you could make? If so, you are in good company. Moses, Esther, Jeremiah, and many others wondered the same thing. And now Millie found herself asking the question, "What possible difference could a twelve-year-old make in a frontier town?"

Do you have doubts that you can make a difference in your home, school, church, neighborhood, or world? If so, describe these doubts below.

 **A pioneer for God must overcome doubt.**

When God begins to reveal His plans for you, you may have doubts or wonder how God could possibly use you. That's how Millie felt. She couldn't see God's big picture for her life. But the fact was that Millie was God's precious work of art. There was no other person like her. She was unique and special, and God had unique and special designs for her life.

Read the following passage from Psalm 139:13–16:

> For you created my inmost being; you knit me together in my mother's womb. I praise you because I am fearfully and wonderfully made; your works are wonderful, I know that full well. My frame was not hidden from you when I was made in the secret place. When I was woven together in the depths of the earth, your eyes saw my unformed body. All the days ordained for me were written in your book before one of them came to be.

How can Psalm 139:13–16 help you overcome any doubts about your uniqueness? Underline all parts of the passage that show that God has intimately designed us.

The last sentence says, "All the days ordained for me were written in your book before one of them came to be." God has good works prepared just for you. You can believe this to be true, because God is faithful to His Word. He is trustworthy.

> " *I* want to give You my hopes and dreams," [Millie prayed]. "I want You to have my future, Jesus. Please, please do something amazing with it!"
>
> —From *Millie's Unsettled Season*, page 48

Millie's doubts about her usefulness in God's Kingdom were changing! At the beginning of this lesson we read how Millie wondered what difference she could make in Pleasant Plains. But now her perspective (viewpoint) was beginning to change. Instead of doubt, Millie was beginning to have faith that God could do something amazing with her future.

Faith is the opposite of _____.

To overcome _____ you must increase your _____.

But how do you increase your faith to overcome your doubts? Look up Romans 10:17 and see what it says about faith. Complete the missing words in the verse below.

Consequently, _____ comes from hearing the _____, and the message is

_____ through the _____ of Christ.

Your faith will increase the more you expose yourself to the Bible, which is the Word of Christ. That's why it is so important to take time to read your Bible, pray, and stay connected to a strong body of believers—your church family.

 **Remember, we're on a lifelong journey. It's a process. You will find as you are growing in your walk with God, that your faith will be growing with you.**

How often do you read your Bible (including devotion books, study guides, etc.)?

- A) 1-3 times a week or less
- B) 3-5 times a week
- C) 5-7 times a week
- D) Most every day

My prayer time is best described as:

- A) Non-existent
- B) Just going through the motions
- C) Mediocre, I know I could give more time to it
- D) Growing and getting more consistent

My general attitude about God is:

- A) He is going to punish me if I do something wrong
- B) I wonder if He is really there
- C) He fascinates me—I truly love Him and wish I knew more of Him
- D) I believe in Him and want to do right, but I don't always understand how to do it

Millie made a habit of reading her Bible most every day when she became a Christian. And we know from the books that she talked to God through prayer all throughout her day. She also had a strong group of godly people she could turn to for support, encouragement, fellowship, and strength. They helped her grow in her relationship with God.

Write down the names of people who can help you grow in your walk with God and offer you support, encouragement, fellowship, and strength:

Pause for a moment and reflect on your answers. Be honest with yourself. Do you feel like you need to spend more time in the Word? What about your prayer life? Is it growing? What about your attitude toward God? Is it something you need to talk over with someone you trust? And look at your list of friends—do you need to reach out and connect with more people in the body of Christ? Ask the Lord to speak to your heart. Write your thoughts below:

If you struggle with believing God's plans for your life, you can overcome your doubts by increasing your faith, which happens when you hear the truths and promises in God's Word. Make it a priority to tackle your doubts by renewing your mind with God's truths.

Fill in the blanks for Ephesians 2:10, this chapter's memory verse:

For we are God's _____, created in Christ Jesus to do _____ _____, which God prepared ___ _____ for us to do.

From memory, write down Proverbs 3:5–6, the memory verse for our entire study:

How do you think your trust in God has grown since beginning this Bible study? (Be specific.)

Godly Role Models

> "A warehouse." Marcia stood for a moment. Millie stood close, and put her arm around her mother's waist. She could feel the tension in her Mamma's muscles, but not a sign of it showed on her face.
>
> "It is a poor place to take you to, my dear," Stuart said, "but it was a 'Hobson's choice,' as I said. There really is no other."
>
> Marcia looked at the building for just one moment more, then stood on tip-toe to kiss her husband's cheek.
>
> "Can't you just imagine Joseph saying that to Mary?" She made her voice deep. "'It's a "Hobson's choice," my dear. This was the only stable available in Bethlehem.' God had a plan for them, Stuart. And He has a plan for us, too."
>
> "We'll soon have our things, everything you need to make it a home," Stuart said, relief obvious in his voice.
>
> "I have everything I need to make it home right here with me," Marcia said, taking his arm. He put his hand over hers and they started on together.
>
> — From *Millie's Unsettled Season*, page 110

It was a critical moment for the Keith family! Imagine the suspense when Stuart led his wife and children toward the run-down warehouse, only to announce that it was their new home! Marcia's reaction would set the tone for the rest of the family. The children looked to her for a response, and in that moment of uncertainty, Marcia could have done one of two things: She could have been disappointed and upset at the rude accommodations, or she could look past it all and make the most of it. She chose to make the most of it! Marcia was a terrific role model for her children. She did not let her emotions take charge of her actions.

 **Whether we realize it or not, people are watching us, and whether we intend it or not, our attitudes and actions will affect others.**

Millie was keenly aware of her mother's initial reaction to the warehouse. Millie could feel the tension in her mother's muscles. But Millie was aware of something else, too. She noticed that her mother did not show any outward signs of disappointment or uncertainty about living in the warehouse. Millie saw how her mother conducted herself in a self-controlled, mature manner. Marcia proved to be a support and encouragement to her husband as well!

Imagine for a moment if Marcia had burst into tears and began despairing over the warehouse and their move to Pleasant Plains. How do you think it would have affected the rest of the family?

Marcia's supportive and positive attitude toward the warehouse set a good example for Millie and the rest of the children.

 **A good role model is someone who has the strength of character to rise above disappointment, fear, or uncertainties, and instead trust in God's plans!**

Who are some of the role models in your life? List them here:

My Role Models	Why They are Important to Me

The next morning, Marcia left the children with Millie and Aunt Wealthy, and met the cleaning woman at what they had begun calling the Big Yellow House. Millie was determined to follow her Mamma's lead and keep a cheerful heart, no matter what happened. As she put A, B, and C's letter in the pocket of her apron, she promised herself that she would not cry, not shed one tear the whole day, no matter what. Had Rebekah cried when she left her family to travel to a distant land and marry Isaac? No. Had Joshua cried when God sent him to take the Promised Land? No. Would Millie Keith shed any more tears for her friends and home? Never! Millie washed her face carefully, and pressed a cool cloth to her still-swollen eyes.

— From *Millie's Unsettled Season*, page 121

Sometimes the role models that God gives us are people who have gone before us. The pioneers of the 1800s depended on the maps, directions, and advice of the people who traveled West before them. The pioneers setting out for the first time needed the experience of the people who made it in order to survive their own journey. In the passage above, what other role models was Millie looking at?

Hebrews chapter 11 lists many godly role models in the faith whose examples all of us can follow. Hebrews 12:1 calls them a "great cloud of witnesses." They have blazed the trail ahead of us. Millie mentioned, for example, Rebekah and Joshua. Their courage in the Lord gave Millie a fresh resolve to stand firm. Can you think of any other people in the Bible who you can look to as role models? Write down some of your favorites and make a brief note as to why they are your favorite:

Now, look at all the people you have listed as role models. What characteristics do you admire most about these people? List at least six things you greatly admire about these role models:

1)   3)   5)

2)   4)   6)

What are some of their notable character traits, especially those to which you might aspire?

In the New Testament we can find many verses that encourage us to imitate the faith and actions of Christian role models in our lives. Let's look at some in the following activity.

Match the verse to the correct Scripture:

1) 1 Corinthians 11:1

2) Hebrews 6:12

3) Hebrews 13:7

4) 3 John 11

5) Philippians 4:9

A) "Dear friends, do not imitate what is evil but what is good. Anyone who does what is good is from God. Anyone who does what is evil has not seen God."

B) "Remember your leaders, who spoke the word of God to you. Consider the outcome of their way of life and imitate their faith."

C) "Whatever you have learned or received or heard from me, or seen in me—put it into practice. And the God of peace will be with you."

D) "Follow my example, as I follow the example of Christ."

E) "We do not want you to become lazy, but to imitate those who through faith and patience inherit what has been promised."

Your role models, whether they are people of the Bible, your parents, or other mature Christians, have one thing in common—they have gone before you. Older Christians have had experiences that can help you.

It's good to have peers to talk to (friends your age who share your faith), but it's important to have older, more mature role models to turn to. Since they have gone before you, they can give you a godly perspective that a peer your own age cannot.

In your own words, describe why it is important to have godly role models in your life:

If you have younger brothers, sisters, cousins, or friends, did you know you could be a role model? Millie had younger siblings and they looked up to her, even if she wasn't always aware of it.

> "It's horrid!" The words were out of Millie's mouth before she could stop them. "How can Pappa expect our Mamma to live there? It isn't a house at all…"
>
> "Millie's right," Zillah said. "This isn't a house! How'll we ever live in it? I want my own room!"
>
> — From *Millie's Unsettled Season*, pages 111, 113

When Millie saw their new home, the warehouse, she was not at all pleased with it. As a matter of fact, she had somewhat of a bad attitude about it, which she voiced. Little Zillah picked up on Millie's displeasure and followed her example. Even though Millie really didn't know it, she was making an impression on her little sister.

Can you think of a time when you made an impression on your younger siblings (or on a younger friend, cousin, etc.) for good or for bad? Briefly describe your experience:

You can also be a role model for your peers and friends. Millie made quite an impression on her new friend, Claudina, at the girls' Bible study:

> *W*hen the other girls had left, Millie turned to Claudina. "I am so sorry," she said. "It was a perfectly lovely afternoon and I spoiled it."
>
> "I will admit we have never had a Bible study quite like that before," Claudina said. "But I don't think you said anything wrong. How can you study the Bible and not speak the truth? Besides, I know Helen and Lu. They will have forgotten about it by tomorrow." She walked Millie to the door.
>
> "I want to apologize to you, Millie," she said. "I knew you were right, and I didn't stand up for you. I am so envious of your courage!"
>
> — From *Millie's Unsettled Season*, page 167

Claudina immediately recognized Millie's commitment to the truth of God's Word, and she admired it. Millie was somewhat of a role model that day. Proverbs 27:17 says, "As iron sharpens iron, so one man sharpens another."

 **Everyone needs godly role models to sharpen them and point them in the right direction.**

Jesus is our ultimate role model and teacher. We should always look to Him and model our lives after His. After all, even Jesus had a role model which He imitated: "I tell you the truth, the Son can do nothing by himself; he can do only what he sees his Father doing, because whatever the Father does the Son also does" (John 5:19).

Our memory verse for this chapter says, "For we are God's workmanship, created in Christ Jesus to do good works, which God prepared in advance for us to do" (Ephesians 2:10).

 **The "good works" which God has prepared for you to do will sharpen and shape the lives of those around you.**

Courage for the Adventure

> *A*unt Wealthy has more courage than anyone I have ever known, Millie thought. Courage enough to face a lion, or even to spend an evening listening to poor Mr. Tittlebaum.
>
> — From *Millie's Courageous Days*, page 32

You might not realize it, but adventures (and the "good works" God has prepared for us!) are not for the fainthearted—they require courage. Without courage it is hard to face an adventure, let alone all the adventures of life.

Describe a time in your life where you had to have courage to do something.

Why did you have courage in that situation?

In what way did you grow as a person or in your walk with God as a result of your stepping out courageously?

The dictionary tells us that courage is defined as mental or moral strength to venture, persevere, and withstand danger, fear, or difficulty. Courage is the strength to overcome obstacles.

Have you ever thought about why some people have a lot of courage while others do not? What is the secret behind their courage? Well, one thing is *trust*. When people have a lot of trust in themselves, or in other people, or even in their circumstances, they often find the courage to do things they would otherwise not be willing to do. Millie really trusted Aunt Wealthy. Aunt Wealthy's advice and encouragement helped Millie to be courageous when times got tough. Millie also trusted her parents.

Who are some of the people in your life that you trust?

In what ways and for what kinds of things do you trust them?

Why do you trust them?

What does your trust in them give you courage to do?

Trustworthy people in our lives can encourage us to be strong and courageous. But only a true trust in God will give us the courage we need to face this adventure called life.

We need to depend on and trust others, but never more than we trust in the Lord. Even our most "trusted" family member or friend will eventually let us down because nobody is perfect. But we *know* that God is good all the time. Therefore we can trust Him to never forsake or fail us.

Most people know the story of David and Goliath. Here is an excerpt from 1 Samuel 17:45–47:

> David said to the Philistine, "You come against me with sword and spear and javelin, but I come against you in the name of the LORD Almighty, the God of the armies of Israel, whom you have defied. This day the LORD will hand you over to me, and I'll strike you down and cut off your head. Today I will give the carcasses of the Philistine army to the birds of the air and the beasts of the earth, and the whole world will know that there is a God in

Israel. All those gathered here will know that it is not by sword or spear that the LORD saves; for the battle is the LORD's, and he will give all of you into our hands."

What gave David his courage to fight Goliath?

In Psalm 44:6–7, David said, "I do not trust in my bow, my sword does not bring me victory; but you [Lord] give us victory over our enemies, you put our adversaries to shame."

David trusted that God's presence and power would be with him! That was the key to David's unusual courage. David also said, "Some trust in chariots and some in horses, but we trust in the name of the LORD our God" (Psalm 20:7).

In our day, where we no longer have real chariots and horses, "chariots and horses" represent worldly strength and power.

As Christians we need to put our trust in the name of the Lord, not in worldly strength and power.

When our trust is in God, we cannot be let down. This is not so when we trust in things other than God.

As an example, one kind of "chariot and horse" could be money. Some people put their trust in money and riches, which carries no guarantee of security or happiness. If their money is stolen or their business closes down, they are left with nothing. "Cast but a glance at riches, and they are gone, for they will surely sprout wings and fly off to the sky like an eagle," says Proverbs 23:5.

Another "chariot and horse" might be popularity or outward beauty. But popularity does not last and outward beauty fades away, so they will certainly let us down.

Charm is deceptive, and beauty is fleeting; but a woman who fears the LORD is to be praised. (Proverbs 31:30)

Even intelligence or wisdom, if it is not God's wisdom, will fail us.

Do not deceive yourselves. . . . For the wisdom of this world is foolishness in God's sight. As it is written: "He catches the wise in their craftiness"; and again, "The LORD knows that the thoughts of the wise are futile. (1 Corinthians 3:18–20)

Can you think of some "chariots and horses" that you have falsely trusted in? If so, list them here:

How did putting your trust in them disappoint you?

Remember, only God will never fail us. If we are placing our trust anywhere else, we will end up disappointed.

 **Only God is truly trustworthy and reliable, and you can trust that His presence will be with you continually.**

Joshua was given a very big task. God wanted him to lead the Israelites into the land of Canaan and wipe out all the powerful inhabitants of the land. God understood this would cause Joshua anxiety and fear.

Read carefully Joshua 1:7–9. What was the promise God gave Joshua to eliminate his fear?

What was the requirement Joshua had to fulfill to obtain success?

There are two important principles we can draw from this passage concerning courage:

1) If we are committed to following the Lord, obeying Him completely, and doing what is right, we will have success. We do not need to fear defeat.

2) God promised Joshua that He would be with him wherever he went. Therefore, knowing God was with him, every step of the way, Joshua could be courageous.

Are you willing to do what is good and pleasing to God æ no matter what? Let boldness arise in your heart knowing God is with you and will grant you success. "The wicked man flees though no one pursues, but the righteous are as bold as a lion." (Proverbs 28:1) "When I called, you answered me; you made me bold and stouthearted." (Psalm 138:3)

Look back over this chapter. Ask the Holy Spirit to show you the most important things He wants you to remember. Put a star beside those truths and, in your own words, summarize below what He showed you.

Rewrite your thoughts as a prayer, asking God to help you grow and apply the truths He's taught you throughout the chapter.

Write out the memory verse for this chapter, Ephesians 2:10:

Write out the memory verse for our entire study, Proverbs 3:5–6:

CHAPTER

4

Hearing God's Voice

Lesson 1
Preparing to Hear God

Lesson 2
The Attitude of a Listener

Lesson 3
Godly Counsel

Lesson 4
Hearing God Through His Word

Lesson 5
*Sensing God Through
the Holy Spirit*

Hearing God's Voice

by heart

The LORD confides in those who fear him; he makes his covenant known to them.   — PSALM 25:14

Preparing to Hear God

"Listen to that!" Aunt Wealthy exclaimed suddenly. "Isn't it marvelous!"

Millie turned her head, listening for the sound, but everything was winter silent. Even the clang of Gordon's hammer was still. "I don't hear a thing."

"That's what's so marvelous. Solitude!"

Millie looked at her aunt's peaceful face, which was upturned toward the sun. How hard it must be for her to live in a house full of children, with curtains for walls. Sound carried right through the fabric, and from the moment the Keiths had set foot in the warehouse, the only quiet times had been when the children were in bed asleep.

"Thank you for asking me to come with you," Millie said.

"You looked as if you could use some solitude yourself," Aunt Wealthy smiled. "I find it much easier to talk to God when I am all alone."

—From *Millie's Courageous Days*, pages 58–59

Have things ever gotten so noisy or crazy at your house that you felt like Aunt Wealthy and just needed to get away so you could hear God? Aunt Wealthy knew the value of a little solitude. Getting alone with God was one way she found to connect with Him. God speaks to us in many ways. By hearing His voice and following Him, we learn to trust Him.

In this chapter we are going to look at many different ways we can hear God's voice in our lives. We'll examine how we can prepare our hearts to hear God and what kind of attitude a listener must have. We will learn the different ways God can speak to us, including through other people, through His Word, and through the Holy Spirit. This chapter will show you how exciting it is to hear the voice of your Shepherd!

Jesus said in John 10 that He is the Shepherd and we are His flock:

> The watchman opens the gate for him, and the sheep listen to his voice. He calls his own sheep by name and leads them out. When he has brought out all his own, he goes on ahead of them, and his sheep follow him because they know his voice. (v. 3–4)

Do you know God's voice in *your* life? When we know the voice of our Shepherd, we can fully trust Him and follow Him wherever He may lead us. For Millie, she found herself following her Shepherd all the way to Pleasant Plains! But before we can follow God anywhere, we must know His voice. We must develop the heart of a listener.

Do you find it hard to listen for God's voice? Explain.

Living in a house with curtains for walls meant that there were many distractions and few quiet moments for the Keith family. Your house might not have curtains for walls, but there are plenty of other things to distract you from quiet moments with the Lord. There are many "noises" in our lives that can hinder us from hearing God's voice. Check any of the following "noises" that get in your way of hearing God:

❏ Television   ❏ Busy Social Life   ❏ Computer/Email   ❏ Telephone

❏ Music   ❏ Radio   ❏ Fatigue   ❏ Activities

❏ Magazines   ❏ Movies   ❏ Siblings   ❏ Other_____

We really do need to prepare to hear God. Aunt Wealthy prepared by getting out of the noisy house to take a quiet walk. One way you might prepare is by turning off the TV and going to your room for a quiet time. Preparing to hear God simply means turning down the volume of the other voices planting seeds in your soul (like television, music, etc.), and getting some quiet time alone with God.

What are some specific things you need to do in your life to prepare to hear God?

Choosing to spend time alone with God instead of watching TV, reading a magazine, or talking on the phone, can be a tough choice. It really boils down to one thing—do you *want* to hear God speak to you?

List the top five priorities in your life right now. (Hint: think about how you spend your time. This will help reveal your priorities.)

1.

2.

3.

4.

5.

If you desire to hear God's voice, you must make it a priority to spend time with Him and learn about who He is. You've got to *want* to hear Him. You must take time each day to tune out everything else and just listen for God.

Making time to be alone with God is an important way to hear His voice, but it isn't the *only* way you can hear Him speak to you. In the following lessons we'll explore other ways God speaks to us. But the common denominator is that a heart that longs to hear God's voice must be prepared to hear His voice.

We can prepare ourselves to hear God by confessing our sins and asking the Lord to cleanse our hearts.

Psalm 66:18–20 says, "If I had cherished sin in my heart, the LORD would not have listened; but God has surely listened and heard my voice in prayer. Praise be to God, who has not rejected my prayer or withheld his love from me!"

Why do you think confessing your sins is important for hearing God's voice?

God is eager to speak to you. He has many tender words for your ears to hear. Look up Isaiah 50:4–5 and complete the missing words in the verse below:

The Sovereign LORD has given me an instructed _____, to know the word that

_____ the weary. He wakens me _____ by morning, wakens

my _____ to _____ like one being taught. The Sovereign LORD has

_____ my ears, and I have not been _____; I have not drawn

back.

Based on this Scripture, what will the Lord teach you if you don't draw away from Him?

This passage says that God will "waken your ears to listen like one being taught." God wants to pour into you. He wants to equip you to speak with wisdom. He wants to give you words that can encourage others.

Write out Psalm 25:14, our memory verse for this chapter.

Look up the word *confide* in your dictionary and write the definition below.

 **God will confide in those whose hearts are ready and prepared to hear from Him! Prepare your heart to hear from God by getting "still" before Him.**

A heart that is "still" can more easily hear from God. Psalm 46:10 says, "Be still, and know that I am God." To "be still" means to be calm, to lay aside worries and distractions, to quiet your soul. As 1 Peter 5:7 tells us, "Cast all your anxiety on him because he cares for you."

Still your heart now and ask your Heavenly Father to help you hear His voice with more clarity. Allow a few minutes of silence and enjoy God's presence. Write down any thoughts or feelings after your time with Him.

The Attitude of a Listener

"Mamma, I am so disgusted with myself. I know I couldn't sleep!"
"Why, Millie, what's wrong?"
Millie explained about the torn book and her harsh words with Cyril.
"I'm sorry about your book," Marcia said. "I didn't know they had caused such destruction."
"It was easy to forgive Don and Fan because they said they were sorry, and I know they meant it," Millie said. "But I haven't forgiven Cyril yet. It wasn't wrong to be angry, I know. But I haven't forgiven him, and that is a sin. The Bible says, 'Be angry, but do not sin. Do not let the sun go down while you are still angry.' The sun has been down a long time, and I am still so angry! I don't know what to do!" Millie knelt and laid her head in her mother's lap.
— From *Millie's Unsettled Season*, pages 46–47

Remember how Millie struggled to forgive her younger brother Cyril for tearing her *Ivanhoe* book? In the above passage we see how Millie finally turned to her mother after many days of harboring unforgiveness toward Cyril. Millie knew her behavior and attitude toward her brother weren't right. It's never easy to share your struggles with someone. It took courage for Millie to confess her sins to her mother. But Millie really wanted freedom from her anger and she was seeking answers. When Millie admitted her sin, her heart was finally soft enough for her to hear from her Shepherd.

When we seek to hear the voice of our Shepherd, we must consider our attitude. God's Word has some specific truths about the kind of attitude a child of God should possess. When we approach God with a right attitude, we can hear God much clearer.

 **The attitude of a listener is one who is humble, teachable, and has a soft, reverent, obedient heart toward God.**

What does it mean to be humble? A humble person is not proud or arrogant. Rather, she is courteous, respectful, modest, meek, gentle, and submissive. Some people see humility as a weakness, but it is really quite the opposite. It takes strength of character to walk in humility. Millie had a humble heart when she went to her mother and confessed her sins.

 **Having an attitude of humility helps make your heart soft to hear God's voice.**

Ask yourself honestly, "Do I have a humble heart?" Allow God to speak to you. Write your thoughts below:

Jesus had a humble heart. He said, "Take my yoke upon you and learn from me, for I am gentle and humble in heart, and you will find rest for your souls" (Matthew 11:29).

The Bible teaches that God loves those whose hearts are humble. Let's look at this further. Look up the following verses and complete the missing words in the verses below:

1) This is the one I _____: he who is _____ and _____ in spirit, who _____ at my word. (Isaiah 66:2)

2) You _____ the _____ but bring _____ those whose eyes are _____. (Psalm 18:27)

3) He _____ the _____ in what is right and _____ them his way. (Psalm 25:9)

From these verses, write down what God offers for those who are humble at heart:

Another important attitude of a listener is one who is teachable. Have you ever known someone who always has an answer to everything and who resists any type of instruction or advice? That's a person who does not have a teachable spirit. If we are to hear God's voice in our lives, we must remain teachable. God has a lot to show us, and if we resist His instruction, we have ears that do not hear. Proverbs 1:23 says, "If you had responded to my rebuke, I would have poured out my heart to you and made my thoughts known to you." We must be open to instruction and correction. Millie's heart was teachable. She embraced the wisdom of her family, and she especially took to heart the words of Scripture. Millie sought out answers to her problems. She was eager to hear from God.

Proverbs 2:1–8 says, "My son, if you accept my words and store up my commands within you, turning your ear to wisdom and applying your heart to understanding, and if you call out for insight and cry aloud for understanding, and if you look for it as for silver and search for it as for hidden treasure, then you will understand the fear of the LORD and find the knowledge of God. For the LORD gives wisdom, and from his mouth come knowledge and understanding. He holds victory in store for the upright, he is a shield to those whose walk is blameless, for he guards the course of the just and protects the way of his faithful ones."

Go back through the passage and underline in one color of ink the words that describe what you should do. We'll get you started on the first two: My son if you <u>accept</u> my words and <u>store up</u> my commands within you . . . Then in a second color of ink underline what God will do for you: For the Lord <u>gives wisdom</u>.

Why do you think it is important to have a teachable heart?

Zechariah 7:11–13—But they refused to pay attention; stubbornly they turned their backs and stopped up their ears. They made their hearts as hard as flint and would not listen to the law or to the words that the LORD Almighty had sent by his Spirit through the earlier prophets. So the LORD Almighty was very angry. "When I called, they did not listen; so when they called, I would not listen," says the LORD Almighty.

Psalm 119:60 — I will hasten and not delay to obey your commands.

God loves a teachable heart—one that is quick to pay attention and obey God.

Last but not least, the heart of a listener fears the Lord. This is perhaps the most important quality of all, for Scripture says that "the fear of the LORD is the beginning of wisdom" (Proverbs 9:10).

Our memory verse for this chapter is Psalm 25:14. Write it down below:

To have the fear of the Lord is to have a deep reverence for Him.

To have the fear of the Lord means to have a sense of awe about who He is and the power that He has. You might have heard the expression, "God is worthy of our praise." But have you ever thought that God, and *only* God, is worthy of our fear? The psalmist declared, "You alone are to be feared. Who can stand before you when you are angry?" (Psalm 76:7).

We can fear so many things in our world today. But the only thing that we should really fear is God Himself. When we have a healthy fear of God, God speaks to us. He will confide in you when you understand what it means to fear (revere) Him.

What are some things that you are afraid of? Record them below with the reasons why you fear them.

My Fears	Reasons Why I Fear These Things

Psalm 145:19 promises, "He fulfills the desires of those who fear him; he hears their cry and saves them." Many things in life are uncertain. But if you trust God and fear only Him, you can say with confidence, "The LORD is my helper; I will not be afraid. What can man do to me?" (Hebrews 13:6).

Take a moment now and ask God to give you a greater portion of the "fear of the Lord."

Let's review the qualities you can possess to help you hear your Shepherd's voice:

The attitude of a listener is one who is <u>humble</u>, <u>teachable</u>, and <u>fears God.</u>

Godly Counsel

*M*arcia stroked her daughter's hair for a moment before she spoke. "You were angry because Cyril tore a book that was very precious to you," she said.

Millie nodded.

"I think you need to give your book away," said Marcia.

"Not to Cyril!" Millie sat up.

"No," said her mother smiling. "Not to Cyril. Give it to Jesus. Then ask yourself if He would forgive Cyril for tearing His book. If you give Him the things that are precious to you, you will be surprised what He can do with them."

"Mamma, that's not all." Millie's voice didn't want to work, but she forced herself to explain how she had pinched her brother.

"You have taken the first step, Millie mine," said Marcia. "Sins have a hold on you if you keep them hidden inside. The Bible tells us to confess our sins to each other and pray for each other so that we may be healed. I am glad you confessed to me. . . ."

"Jesus," [Millie] prayed, "Mamma said that You could do amazing things if I give You the things that are precious to me. So...I want You to have this book. You can do anything You want with it. And...and I want to give You my hopes and dreams, too. I want You to have my future, Jesus. Please, please do something amazing with it!"

— From *Millie's Unsettled Season*, page 47

Millie knew that her mother was someone she could turn to for wisdom. God spoke to Millie through her mother and through other important people in her life, like her father and Aunt Wealthy.

 **One way God will speak to you is through trusted authority figures in your life, especially your parents.**

How has God spoken to you through your parents in the past?

Has God spoken to you through any other trusted adults? Who? Give examples.

Look at each of these verses:

Proverbs 6:20–22 — My son, keep your father's commands and do not forsake your mother's teaching. Bind them upon your heart forever; fasten them around your neck. When you walk, they will guide you; when you sleep, they will watch over you; when you awake, they will speak to you.

Proverbs 12:15 — The way of a fool seems right to him, but a wise man listens to advice.

Proverbs 15:22 — Plans fail for lack of counsel, but with many advisers they succeed.

Why do you think it's important to embrace the wisdom of your parents and other spiritual leaders in your life?

In the last lesson we learned that we must be humble and teachable to receive from God. These same attitudes will also enable us to receive wisdom from others. "Let the wise listen and add to their learning, and let the discerning get guidance," says Proverbs 1:5.

Can you remember a time when you were not teachable—when you were unwilling to receive guidance given by your parents or other respected adults? For example, when you got mad at them for not allowing you to do something you wanted to do. What was the fruit, or result, of not having a teachable spirit?

Our verse for this chapter is Psalm 25:14. Complete the missing words in the verse below:

The LORD _____ in those who _____ him; he makes his _____

known to them.

 **God will use the counsel of others in our lives to direct our steps.**

"$\mathcal{M}$amma, how does God answer you when you pray?"
"Well," Marcia replied, snipping the end of her thread. "Sometimes He talks to me as I am reading my Bible—a verse just stands out. At other times, He brings a Scripture that I have memorized to mind. Sometimes He speaks to me through your father, who is a very wise and godly man. Sometimes it takes a long time, and sometimes," she exchanged a knowing look with Wealthy, "it doesn't. He seems to have answered Pappa's prayer about the house already."
—From *Millie's Unsettled Season*, page 37

The counsel of others is one way God speaks to us. In the excerpt above, what are all the different ways mentioned? List them here.

On your list above, put a check next to the ways you have had God speak to you.

Hearing God Through His Word

Millie awoke in the gray of the morning and crept quietly out of her berth. She slipped into her clothes, picked up her Bible, and made her way up to the deck…. She leaned against the bulwark and watched as the sun came up like a fiery ball out of the lake. There was still no breath of wind. She had a few precious moments to read. She had been in the habit of reading her Bible at least once a day since she had become a Christian two years before. Pappa had knelt with her when she prayed to accept Jesus as her Lord, and then he had given her his own Bible. It had been worn then, but it was positively tattered now. Millie had carried the book with her not only to church and to school, but up trees and under hedges—all of her favorite reading places. Now, it showed the wear and tear of this trip, too, but Millie didn't care.

— From *Millie's Unsettled Season*, page 83

Millie had a lot of questions about God, more questions than answers! Millie's faith was growing and she often struggled on her journey toward Christian maturity. She still had much to learn about trusting God and hearing His voice, like we all do! But one thing Millie was committed to was reading her Bible. Millie knew that the only way she would grow in her relationship with God was to spend time with Him and study His Word.

 **God will confide in us through His Word.**

Sometimes reading the Bible and hearing God through His Word can seem hard. But it really just takes practice. For instance, if you play a musical instrument, what did you do the first time you tried to play it and it didn't sound very good? Or what about when you looked at the sheet music for the first time and it didn't make any sense? Did you give up the instrument because it was too hard to learn? Of course not! Instead, you took lessons, practiced at home, learned the notes, and your skill level grew and grew! Perhaps you can now play your instrument pretty well, but you probably still practice and take lessons to get even better.

Well, hearing God by reading the Bible is no different. If you've tried to read it in the past and it just didn't make any sense, or you couldn't hear God speaking to you, don't give up! It takes practice! And the more you practice at it, the easier it becomes to hear your Shepherd's voice.

There are things you can do to help you "practice" reading the Bible. For example, you might consider finding an older woman to help mentor (or teach) you through a book of the Bible.

Millie had many ways of practicing reading the Bible. For one thing she spent time alone reading God's Word every day. That was a priority in her life. Millie also participated in group Bible studies and enjoyed listening to Reverend Lord's sermons on Sunday mornings. Bible discussion was also a part of Millie's home life too. Many times Millie's family would read the Bible together and discuss the passages. These are all great ways to get into the Word and hear God's voice!

 **God's Word is alive — therefore it speaks to our hearts!**

Hebrews 4:12 says, "For the word of God is living and active. Sharper than any double-edged sword, it penetrates even to dividing soul and spirit, joints and marrow; it judges the thoughts and attitudes of the heart." When we open up God's Word, we should anticipate something happening in our hearts because the Word is alive! Millie experienced the thrill of God's Word coming to life in the following excerpt:

"$\mathcal{W}$hy, Lord? Why have You brought us to this terrible place? I'm sure I can't bear it. I can't bear it!"

When the tears subsided, Millie picked up her Bible and opened it, intending to read from the book of Psalms, where she often found comfort. The book fell open to the forty-fifth chapter of Isaiah, and as she glanced down, her attention was distinctly drawn to some words on the page. "I will give you the treasures of darkness, riches stored in secret places, so that you may know that I am the Lord, the God of Israel, who summons you by name," read verse 3.

Millie read the words again slowly. They seemed alive somehow, like they were speaking right to her. Millie's heartbeat quickened. *Could this be what Mamma was talking about when she said that sometimes a Scripture just jumps out at her?* Sweet comfort spread through her. *Treasures of darkness? Riches stored in secret places? Why do I suddenly feel such an odd sense of peace?* Millie studied the page in silence.

Lord, this passage is about someone named Cyrus, but are You trying to tell ME something? Millie waited for a reply, but heard none. Still, she wondered, could God have something special for them in this gloomy place? Could there be treasure she couldn't yet see?

> *I'm sorry I was so disappointed in our new house, God. I'm sorry I let my words spill out and make the children disappointed, too. Show me what Your plans are, Lord. Help me be strong. Help me trust You.*
>
> — From *Millie's Unsettled Season*, page 118

Millie was desperate to hear from God. She sought comfort and answers in her little Bible, and God spoke to her! How was God's Word "living and active" to Millie in this passage?

Have you, like Millie, experienced the thrill of God's Word jumping out at you and speaking directly to your heart? If so, describe how it made you feel to have God speak to you. If not, ask the Holy Spirit to open your "spiritual ears and eyes" so that you can understand God's Word. He is your helper in spiritual things (1 John 14:24), as we will see in the next lesson. Write your feelings or request in the space below.

After God spoke to Millie through Isaiah 45, Millie was more attentive to the people and situations around her. She was looking for those "riches stored in secret places." When God speaks to you through the Word, take action. Sometimes it might be instruction, like overcoming anger. Other times it could be a promise, like for Millie, and you can simply be more aware of your surroundings to see what God might be putting together.

Hearing the Word and putting it into practice is a critical part of trusting God.

Is there something heavy on your heart that you'd like to seek God's wisdom for? Write out a prayer asking God to speak to you. Then take time in the next few days to read your Bible and look for ways God might be answering you. You probably won't find the *specific* answer you need, but by finding and applying God's truths to your situation, you will find the wisdom and will of God. Refer to the previous lessons in this chapter as a review for hearing God's voice.

A very important thing to remember when learning to hear God's voice is that God will *never* contradict His Word or His nature. If you feel God is leading you to do anything contrary to who He is or what He has said, you are being deceived.

Recite Proverbs 3:5–6 out loud.

The phrase "lean not on your own understanding" means that we trust in *God's* wisdom, not our own.

We learn God's wisdom by reading the Bible.

Psalm 119:97–104:

Oh, how I love your law! I meditate on it all day long. Your commands make me wiser than my enemies, for they are ever with me. I have more insight than all my teachers, for I meditate on your statutes. I have more understanding than the elders, for I obey your precepts. I have kept my feet from every evil path so that I might obey your word. I have not departed from your laws, for you yourself have taught me. How sweet are your words to my taste, sweeter than honey to my mouth! I gain understanding from your precepts; therefore I hate every wrong path.

From that passage, what are the rewards of keeping and learning God's Word?

We hear God when we read the truth found in the Psalms or Proverbs. We hear God when we read about Abraham, Daniel, and Jesus. We hear God when we read the letters of Paul in the New Testament. We hear God in all of His Word.

Every word, every prayer, and every story in the Bible is God's way of speaking to you.

Open up your Bible and discover the beautiful voice of your Lord, for He is calling you to Him!

Sensing God Through the Holy Spirit

> *M*illie had not felt more kindness or hospitality in any home in Pleasant Plains. When the others offered her tea, she knew they had plenty for themselves. The Lightcaps were giving her their best, all they had. *I will give you the treasures of darkness, riches stored in secret places . . . .* Millie drew in her breath as she remembered. *Could the Lightcaps be the riches God promised? They certainly are hidden in darkness!*
> —From *Millie's Unsettled Season*, page 218

In the last lesson we learned how God really does speak to us through the Bible! The Word is living and active and we should anticipate great things when we open our hearts and open up God's Word. The Word came alive to Millie when she was desperate to hear from God about why He sent them to Pleasant Plains. When Millie turned to Isaiah 45, something great happened—the Word came to life and God began speaking to her about why she was there! After that, Millie took action. She began looking for the hidden treasures that God spoke of.

It wasn't until some time later when the passage from Isaiah 45 began to make more sense to Millie. It was as if another piece to her puzzle was fitting into place. Something inside of Millie began to reveal new understanding or insight — Millie was sensing that the Lightcaps were the riches God promised!

The Holy Spirit quickens to our minds the Word buried inside our hearts.

That *something* inside of Millie was God's Holy Spirit. Jesus called the Holy Spirit our "Counselor." In John 14:24 Jesus said, "But the Counselor, the Holy Spirit, whom the Father will send in my name, will teach you all things and will remind you of everything I have said to you." The Holy Spirit reminded Millie what God had said to her through the passage in Isaiah. We can rely on and trust in God's Holy Spirit to speak to us and reveal God's truth in our lives.

Trust in the Holy Spirit to be your helper in hearing God.

The Holy Spirit works in our lives by helping us remember God's Word hidden in our hearts. That's why it's important to read the Word, so that the Holy Spirit can teach us. Can you remember a time when you were reminded of a Scripture verse and you were comforted by it or were able to encourage someone with it? Write down your experience:

Let's look at another example of how the Holy Spirit spoke to Millie. Remember when Millie and her family were on the ship sailing to Pleasant Plains and Cyril got head lice? Well, God spoke to Millie through His Holy Spirit. If you recall, Millie was still upset with Cyril for ripping her *Ivanhoe* book. But God used the following situation to speak to Millie about her attitude toward her brother:

"Itchy head, bugs in bed!" a girl called, scratching her head and laughing. "Bet you're gonna wish you're dead!"

"That's very bad grammar," Millie said, starting toward the girl. How dare she tease that way! Cyril hadn't done anything wrong. He just didn't think about what he was doing.

The little girl ran to the back of the boat where her mother was sitting, and Millie stopped where she was. She turned and almost ran down the steps to the cabin. She rooted through her carpetbag until she found *Ivanhoe*, opened it to the picture of Rebecca, and ran her finger down the tear. *Cyril just didn't think.*

She took the book up onto the deck, and settled into the shade by her brothers.

"Don't yell at us anymore, please, Millie," Don said. "We can't stand it. We're sorry about the picture."

"I wasn't going to yell," Millie said. "I was going to read to you."

— From *Millie's Unsettled Season*, pages 66–67

The Holy Spirit will help you make "connections" in your mind. Circumstances may seem to fit together like puzzle pieces, or the Holy Spirit might remind you of something from the past at the precise moment that it will help you in the present.

When the girl made fun of Cyril for his lice, Millie said to herself that Cyril didn't do anything wrong, he just didn't think about what he was doing. Then, bam! The Holy Spirit instantly helped Millie make a connection about Cyril's similar behavior with her book — he just didn't think. This helped Millie to forgive her brother and better understand the circumstance. Cyril didn't harm her book on purpose. Millie was able to read the book to the children to make Don and Cyril feel better about their shaved heads.

When has the Holy Spirit helped you see into a situation to help you make the right "connections"?

Sometimes Scriptures will just pop into your mind to help you in difficult circumstances. This is another way the Holy Spirit helps us to hear God. This happened to Millie when Gordon was injured:

"**W**e're going to have to pull it out, of course," Dr. Chetwood said at last, "but it is very close to the heart, Gordon. It's going to be risky."

"No," Gordon whispered as Dr. Chetwood touched the rod.

"I don't have a choice," Dr. Chetwood said.

"Let me die."

Silent tears had been running down Rhoda Jane's cheeks, and now she sobbed out loud.

"No!" Millie said. "Why would you say such a thing?"

Gordon shook his head.

For I am the Lord, your God, who takes hold of your right hand and says to you, Do not fear; I will help you. The verse just came into Millie's brain. *Is that for Gordon, Lord? Should I say it out loud?*

"Just let me die," Gordon repeated.

"For I am the Lord, your God, who takes hold of your right hand and says to you, Do not fear; I will help you." Millie hardly recognized her own voice.

"Is that from the Bible?" Gordon asked.

"Yes," Millie said. She felt terribly shaky inside.

"Where, Millie?" Rhoda Jane pulled the Bible that Millie had given her from the shelf.

"Time is of the essence here," Dr. Chetwood said. "Can't this wait?"

"No," Rhoda Jane said, shoving the Bible at Millie. "It can't." Millie flipped to Isaiah 41:13 and handed it back to her.

"For I am the Lord, your God, who takes hold of your right hand and says to you, Do not fear; I will help you." Rhoda Jane read the words in desperation. "It's right here, Gordy." There were tears running down her face. "It's right here. Let the doctor help you, please!"

Gordon closed his eyes for a moment, then nodded. "All right."

— From *Millie's Courageous Days*, pages 116–117

When Gordon wanted to die rather than have surgery, the "right hand" verse just popped into Millie's mind! Once again, the Holy Spirit was helping Millie speak truth into the lives of others. John 16:13 says, "But when he, the Spirit of truth, comes, he will guide you into all truth. He will not speak on his own; he will speak only what he hears, and he will tell you what is yet to come."

Why do you think it's important to have God's Word hidden in your heart?

As you begin to listen more and more for God's voice in your life, you will begin "sensing" God through the Holy Spirit and realizing that God is at work around you, helping you make connections and helping you remember God's Word in such ways like Scriptures popping into your mind. You will begin to understand that that is hearing God—you are hearing your Shepherd's voice!

Reminders for Hearing God's Voice:

❖ Prepare to hear God by choosing to make time for Him, confessing your sins, and getting "still" before Him.

❖ Adopt the attitude of a listener, which one who is humble, teachable, and has a soft, reverent, obedient heart toward God.

❖ Remember that God speaks to you through trusted authority figures in your life, especially your parents.

❖ God's Word is alive and it speaks to you. We learn God's wisdom by reading the Bible and putting it into practice.

❖ The Holy Spirit helps you to hear God, quickening to your mind the Word buried in your heart and helping you see "connections" that God wants you to see.

Write out Joshua 1:8 in the space below.

What does Joshua 1:8 tell you about *when* you should be thinking about the promises, truths, and commands in God's Word?

Look back over this chapter. Ask the Holy Spirit to show you the most important things He wants you to remember. Put a star beside those truths and, in your own words, summarize below what He showed you.

Rewrite your thoughts as a prayer, asking God to help you grow and apply the truths He's taught you throughout the chapter.

Write out the memory verse for this chapter, Psalm 25:14:

Write out the memory verse for our entire study, Proverbs 3:5–6:

CHAPTER

5

Attitude Check

Lesson 1
A Mixed Bag

Lesson 2
Rotten Apples

Lesson 3
Who's in Charge—You or Your Emotions?

Lesson 4
You Call This Good?

Lesson 5
Looking to Jesus

Attitude Check

by heart

*A*nd we know that in all things God works for the good of those who love him, who have been called according to his purpose.

— ROMANS 8:28

A Mixed Bag

"*M*illie's right," Zillah said. "This isn't a house! How'll we ever live in it? I want my own room!"

Marcia stood in the first upper room, turning from side to side, a look of bewilderment on her face.

Aunt Wealthy, who had pulled the door to heaven shut, saw it and came to the rescue. "Never mind, dear; it will look very different when we have unpacked and arranged your furniture. Do you know that in China they make walls out of paper? With the help of curtains, several rooms can be made out of this, and we'll do nicely."

"No doubt," Marcia answered. "This front room shall be yours."

"No, no! You and Stuart must take this one."

"I'm quite set on having my own way," Marcia said. "It is the best room, and you must take it. Besides, I should be afraid to have the little ones in there with that outside door opening onto nothing."

"We'll nail it shut," Wealthy said, "just in case."

"Well, wife, what do you think?" asked Stuart, coming up the stairs.

"I think it will keep the rain off and the children in," Marcia said. "And it's a great deal nicer than a tent. What more could we ask?"

"I think we could ask for a lot more!" Millie said. "It's a great big dirty barn with plaster all over the floor and spattered on the windows too."

"I hope it can be cleaned," her father said, laughing at her rueful face. "Mrs. Prior can probably tell us where to find a woman to help with it."

Stuart and Marcia seemed determined to discuss plans for the arrangement of the inside of the dwelling, so Millie went back downstairs and stepped outside. The scene had not improved. In one direction she saw only a wall of rough weatherboarding with one window in the second story. In the other direction, a heap of sand and a wilderness of weeds. Behind the house was a small stand of willows and a cow shed. Beyond that, a grassy hillside.

"Could You show me the reason for bringing us here, Lord," Millie said out loud, "because I … I'm dumb with despair!"

"Can dumb folks talk?" Cyril asked, coming up behind her. The family was pouring out the door, like ants from a nest.

"We'll cover it with vines," said Aunt Wealthy, seeing Millie's look.

"And I'll clear the yard and sod it," added Rupert, seizing a great mullein stalk and pulling it up by the roots as he spoke. "Won't be nearly as hard as the clearing the early pioneers of Ohio had to do, our grandfathers among them."

—From *Millie's Unsettled Season*, pages 113–114

So far, we've learned much in our study of "Adventures in Trusting God." We've learned that God is trustworthy, that we need to have a new mindset for the journey, and we've learned ways to hear God's voice in our life. Now we're going to learn that we need to have the right attitude for our adventures with God and why our attitude matters.

Millie's family faced hard changes and difficult circumstances in *Millie's Unsettled Season*. One of the biggest challenges the family faced was when they moved out of their lovely home in Lansdale and into an abandoned warehouse in Pleasant Plains! Each member of the family approached this challenge with differing attitudes and perspectives.

An "attitude" is the way you feel toward a person or thing. Attitudes can be positive, negative, selfish or unselfish, or encouraging to others or discouraging. Our attitudes can change from person to person and situation to situation.

Let's look at the different attitudes Millie's family had about their new home. Re-read the above passage and describe the attitudes of the following people:

Zillah	
Aunt Wealthy	

Marcia	
Stuart	
Millie	
Rupert	

Who had positive attitudes?

Who had negative attitudes?

Now let's look at another attitude — Jesus' attitude.

> Your attitude should be the same as that of Christ Jesus: Who, being in very nature God, did not consider equality with God something to be grasped, but made himself nothing, taking the very nature of a servant, being made in human likeness. And being found in appearance as a man, he humbled himself and became obedient to death — even death on a cross! (Philippians 2:5–8)

Philippians 2:5 says that your attitude should be "the same as that of Christ Jesus." From the verses above, what words would you use to describe Jesus' attitude?

In general, how do you feel your attitude compares with that of Jesus?

Millie said, "Could You show me the reason for bringing us here, Lord, because I'm dumb with despair!" Sometimes it's not easy to have a positive attitude. Millie couldn't hide the disappointment in her heart when she saw what was to be her new home. She felt overwhelmed with despair and saw the home as a setback, not a move forward. But look again at our study guide memory verse, Proverbs 3:5–6. It says, "Trust in the LORD with all your heart and lean not on your own understanding; in all your ways acknowledge him, and he will make your paths straight."

How could this verse have helped Millie overcome her disappointment and bad attitude?

 **When we feel disappointment, anger, selfishness, or any emotion that makes us want to have a negative attitude, we can *choose* to trust in the Lord instead.**

Romans 8:28, our memory verse for this chapter, further adds to the promise of Proverbs 3:5–6. It says, "And we know that *in all things* God works *for the good* of those who love him, who have been called according to his purpose."

 **Even in the most disappointing of circumstances, God is in control. He has a plan and it is good.**

How could Romans 8:28 encourage you during a hard time?

The promise of Romans 8:28 does not apply to everyone. Fill in the following blank:

And we know that in all things God works for the good of _____

_____, who have been called according to his purpose.

Rotten Apples

Millie hung back. The feeling of dread she had experienced upon arriving in Pleasant Plains was not only sinking in, it was taking root in her soul. Stables were perfectly all right for Bible stories. It was nice to think about the baby and the sweet-smelling hay at Christmas time. But this wasn't a Bible story. It was real life. She tried to hold her feelings inside, but they boiled up.

"It's horrid!" The words were out of Millie's mouth before she could stop them. "How can Pappa expect our Mamma to live there? It isn't a house at all. It fronts on the street and the door opens right out onto a sand bank."

"There's a big yard at the side and behind," said Zillah.

"Something green in it, too," added Adah.

"Those are weeds!" The blur of tears in Millie's eyes made the weedy yard swim, looking almost like a garden. If she cried hard enough, this horrible thing might look a little like the home they had left with its large garden and endless flower beds. The June roses and the woodbine must be out by now—the air sweet with their delicious perfume— but they and those who had planted and tended them were far away from this desolate spot. How could she write to her friends that she was living in a warehouse?

"Not a tree, a shrub, a flower, or a blade of grass!" Zillah said.

"Never mind, we'll have lots of flowers next year," said Rupert.

The front door was wide open, as the last load of their household goods had just been brought up from the river, so the Keiths walked right in. The men were carrying in the heavy boxes and setting them down upon the floor of the large room.

"Where's the entry hall?" asked Cyril.

"There isn't any," Zillah said. "No cupboards or closets at all. Just bare walls and windows."

"Don't forget the floor and ceilings," Rupert said. "They are important, too."

"And a door on the other side," said Adah, running across the room and opening it.

"Not a mantelpiece to set anything on, nor any chimney at all! How on earth are we going to keep warm in the wintertime?" Millie asked despairingly.
— From *Millie's Unsettled Season*, pages 111–112

To Millie, everything about Pleasant Plains seemed horrible. She could only see through critical eyes. She was overwhelmed with a rotten attitude.

 **A bad attitude only makes a difficult situation more unbearable.**

How do you think a bad attitude can hurt your walk with God?

 **A bad attitude that is left untreated will hinder your walk with God by undermining your faith and trust in Him and hardening your heart toward Him. This can lead to consequences that you will later regret.**

In Numbers 12, we read about someone who had a bad attitude and the serious consequences that came from it. Moses was given the assignment from God to lead the Israelites out of Egypt and bring them to the land of Canaan, God's chosen land for them to live in. This was not an easy assignment, but it did give Moses a lot of authority. Miriam, Moses's sister, became jealous in her heart and began to criticize her brother. At first she complained about little things, but because she didn't deal with her bad attitudes, it grew worse. Soon she was speaking against Moses with arrogance and rebellion. As we've said, bad attitudes are infectious. God could not allow this foul attitude to spread to the others. There would soon be a wide-scale mutiny against His chosen leader. So the Lord had to deal severely with Miriam and struck her with leprosy for seven days.

Miriam learned a huge lesson about her attitudes. We may not get struck with leprosy, but be assured that our bad attitudes are displeasing to the Lord. If left undealt with, they grow like an infection in our soul and pollute our love, faith, and devotion toward God. Like an infectious disease, it spreads quickly to others.

Bad attitudes stem from unbelief. They deny the truth that God is good and that He can work all things together for good (Romans 8:28). A bad attitude is a signal that your thoughts are not lining up with the Word of God.

Write out our chapter memory verse, Romans 8:28, again.

If you do not believe this promise that God is working His GOOD purpose in your life, you can easily fall prey to bad attitudes. Have you ever noticed that when you let a bad attitude creep into your heart, soon nothing seems good?

Look now at Philippians 2:12–14:

> Therefore, my dear friends, as you have always obeyed—not only in my presence, but now much more in my absence—continue to work out your salvation with fear and trembling, for it is God who works in you to will and to act *according to his good purpose.* Do everything without complaining or arguing….

Do you believe that God is working His *good* and perfect will in your life? If so, can you trust Him with the *negative* things that come your way without responding in a *negative* way? Can you believe He will turn it all for *good?*

The Bible says that the joy of the Lord is our strength (Nehemiah 8:10). The enemy wants us to have negative outlooks in life because a bad attitude robs us of God's joy in our hearts. This causes us to lose our peace, making it hard to trust God and be led by His Holy Spirit into doing the good works He has prepared in advance for us to do (Ephesians 2:10).

You've probably heard the expression, "One bad apple spoils a bunch." Well, it's the same with our attitudes. One person's bad attitude can spoil other people's attitudes.

In the passage at the beginning of this lesson, how did Millie's attitude about their home affect the attitude of Zillah?

People watch and learn from other people. Zillah looked up to Millie, and when she saw Millie's reaction to their home, Zillah reacted the same way. Zillah was affected by Millie's attitude.

Have you ever been affected by a negative attitude of one of your friends, siblings, or family members? How?

Can you think of a time when your negative attitude affected someone else?

Always remember that YOU are a godly role model to someone.

Who's in Charge—You or Your Emotions?

> *M*illie couldn't shake the feeling of wrongness in everything — Fan's stillness, the walls between rooms made of curtains, the tables and chairs made of packing crates. What were the Keiths of Lansdale, Ohio, doing in this place? How could they be living in a warehouse with a door that opened into thin air? Millie knew how she would have answered those questions just a few hours before: *It's all God's will. He has a special plan for us!* But now . . .
>
> —From *Millie's Courageous Days*, page 5

Do you ever have days when it seems like your emotions control your life? Maybe you've awakened "on the wrong side of the bed," and a bad attitude stuck with you all day long? Or you've become so depressed over a trifling friendship problem, that the whole world seems to be falling around you? Emotions are as changeable and fickle as the weather. One minute you can be happy and optimistic, then in a moment, you can be sad and see nothing but the bad in life.

On our journey with God we will have fun and adventure, for sure! But we will also have uncertain times and hardships. That's why we need to learn to recognize our emotions and attitudes and check them against God's perfect truths. Emotions, like attitudes, seem to have a will of their own. They too must be subjected to God's truth.

 **We need to be rooted in God's truths, not in our wavering emotions. How we *feel* about something does not mean it's correct. We must rise above our fickle emotions and choose to believe in God's truth.**

Describe a time when you let your emotions rule your thoughts and behaviors:

You cannot lean on or trust in your emotions because they are not necessarily rooted in truth. Trusting in emotions is like the man described in James 1:6 who is like the surf of the sea driven and tossed by the wind. Or the man in Matthew 7:24 who built his house on sand. It is like being on an emotional roller coaster.

 **Being led by emotions is being led by our sinful, human nature (Romans 8:5–6) instead of being led by the Holy Spirit.**

Romans 8:5–6 says:

> Those who live according to the sinful nature have their minds set on what that nature desires; but those who live in accordance with the Spirit have their minds set on what the Spirit desires. The mind of sinful man is death, but the mind controlled by the Spirit is life and peace; the sinful mind is hostile to God. It does not submit to God's law, nor can it do so. Those controlled by the sinful nature cannot please God.

God desires us to be even-keeled. Psalm 143:10 says, "Teach me to do your will, for you are my God; may your good Spirit lead me on level ground." An even-keeled person is steady and continues to walk in peace despite negative circumstances.

Look at the following excerpts and notice the fickleness of Millie's emotions compared to the steadiness of Aunt Wealthy's peace.

> "So how do you like travel?" Aunt Wealthy asked. "Is it as exciting as you expected?"
>
> "I don't like it at all so far," Millie confessed. "It is cramped and uncomfortable, and I don't know how the children are going to stand days of this. I thought it would be more . . . well, exciting."
>
> "But it is exciting!" exclaimed Aunt Wealthy. "The breeze is so refreshing, the moonlight so beautiful."
>
> — From *Millie's Unsettled Season*, page 58

> Millie awoke in the gray of the morning and crept quietly out of her berth. She slipped into her clothes, picked up her Bible, and made her way up to the deck.
>
> "Good morning, Jesus," she whispered. "Thank You for letting me come on this trip. Maybe I do like adventures after all."
>
> — From *Millie's Unsettled Season*, page 82

Let's look at another excerpt.

> It was a beautiful morning, the air sweet with the smell of honeysuckle. Bees buzzed past the packet, and the birds were creating a riotously joyful noise in the tree tops. The passengers who had been most vociferous about their discomfort the night before, greeted one another almost jovially, the light of the sun seeming to make all the difference in their personalities. *Am I like that, Jesus?* Millie had never thought of it before. Her own Mamma and Pappa and Aunt Wealthy had seemed just as pleasant and polite in the damp crowded dark of the night as they were in the cheerful light of day. It was as if what was inside them could not be changed by the world outside of them. *I want to be like them, Jesus,* Millie prayed. *I want to be constant in Your ways and in Your love.*
>
> — From *Millie's Unsettled Season*, page 62

What did Millie admire in the emotions of her parents and Aunt Wealthy?

Millie's parents and Aunt Wealthy did not let their emotions rule them—they were in charge of their emotions. It would have been easy to complain and despair over the discomfort of their sleeping arrangements (like the other passengers did), but instead they remained constant in God's ways. Their attitudes and emotions were not swayed by what was going on around them because inside their hearts they were anchored to God's truths!

 **When we are anchored to God's truths we cannot be swayed by what's going on around us.**

You Call *This* Good?

Lord [prayed Millie], *weren't You watching over Fan and Cyril and Don? Mamma and Pappa always pray for You to watch over us. Mamma always prays for guardian angels to surround her little ones. Did they forget? Did You bring us to this horrible place so that Fan could die? Aunt Wealthy says that all things work together for the good of those who believe in God....*

"How could this possibly be good?" [Millie later asked Aunt Wealthy]. "I don't think the apostle Paul's little sister was dying when he wrote [Romans 8:28]."

"No," Aunt Wealthy said slowly, "his little sister was not dying. Someday you should read all of chapter eight at once, Millie. Too many people make the mistake of memorizing just that one verse. That chapter has seen me through some very rough times. During the almost fifty years I've been following the Lord, I've laughed and I've sung, but I've hurt a lot too. People I love have died—"

> Millie put her hands over her face, but Aunt Wealthy's arms went around her instantly. "I don't mean that Fan is going to die. I don't know what God will do. But with the exception of Enoch and Elijah, nobody I know of has gotten out of this place without their body dying. God calls us to a wild adventure, not a tea party, my dear. I don't follow Jesus because He can give me a life without pain. I follow Him because He is *good*. Someday I will follow Him right through death, and into our Heavenly Father's house."
> — From *Millie's Courageous Days*, pages 10–11, 16–17

Trusting God. That's not always easy to do when your circumstances are scary and uncertain. Millie knew God's truth in Romans 8:28, that God works for the good of those who love Him. But Millie wondered how Fan's accident and their seemingly disastrous move to Pleasant Plains had anything to do with the "good" God had planned for them! To Millie, it seemed all wrong.

Remember our memory verse in Proverbs 3:5–6. We must not lean on our own understanding of what is "good" for our lives. We must trust in God even though we cannot understand it. God allows pain, sorrow, suffering, and death to be a part of His good plan. This is the part of Romans 8 that Aunt Wealthy was referring to — the part we would rather ignore because we do not understand how it could be "good."

Romans 8:17–18
Now if we are children, then we are heirs—heirs of God and co-heirs with Christ, if indeed we share in his sufferings in order that we may also share in his glory. I consider that our present sufferings are not worth comparing with the glory that will be revealed in us.

 **Our lives as Christians will not be free of suffering and sorrow. Even Jesus suffered so that His eternal purposes could be achieved. God will sometimes allow suffering in your life to achieve His good purposes for you, too. This is why you must trust God and not lean on your own understanding.**

Turn in your Bible to Romans 8:35–39 and complete the verses below.

Romans 8:35–39

Who shall separate us from the _____ of Christ? Shall _____ or

_____ or _____ or famine or nakedness or danger or sword?

As it is written: "For your sake we face death all day long; we are considered as

_____ to be slaughtered." No, in all these things we are more than

_____ through him who loved us. For I am convinced that neither

_____ nor _____, neither _____ nor _____, neither the

_____ nor the _____, nor any _____, neither _____

nor _____, nor anything else in all _____, will be able to

_____ us from the _____ of God that is in Christ Jesus our LORD.

As you were writing, did you see a promise of God revealed in this Scripture? According to this Scripture, what is the promise God has for us in the midst of our suffering?

Read 2 Corinthians 11:24–28 in your Bible. In the space below, list all of the hardships faced by the apostle Paul.

Now write out Romans 8:37 to once again see Paul's viewpoint about his suffering.

Describe a time when your circumstances were beyond your understanding of how God was working for good.

How did the situation affect your emotions and attitudes? Were you sad, angry, or discouraged? Why did you feel that way?

When we trust in the Lord and trust in His understanding of our circumstances (and not our own understanding), we can be sure that God will guide us each day and make our paths straight. Then, when the storms of life hit us and things get hard, we don't have to doubt. Instead, we can go back to God's promise and persevere through the hard times.

 **When we don't understand our circumstances we need to trust God the most. There are things we will understand only *after* we have passed through a situation.**

There are many instances in the Bible when things did not appear "good" until God later revealed the fullness of His plan.

For example, consider the life of Joseph in Genesis chapters 37–47. Joseph was seventeen years old when he was sold as a slave by his brothers to Egyptians. As if it wasn't bad enough that he had lost his family and was a slave in a strange land, next he found himself, through no fault of his own, thrown into prison. No doubt Joseph struggled with doubting that God could turn his situation to good. He was not able to see how God was working good through his situation until many years later at the age of 30 when he was released from prison and promoted to a position second only to Pharaoh. Then the goodness of God's plan was revealed! God not only blessed Joseph personally, but also used Joseph to save a nation of people, including his own race, during a severe drought. We find Joseph proclaiming to his repentant brothers that what they intended for evil God turned around for good. God worked a good and perfect plan in Joseph's life, but Joseph was not able to see it for thirteen years. Yet we can tell by his behavior and his words that he never ceased trusting in God.

Like Joseph, Millie had to learn to trust God and believe that even when her circumstances looked bad, God was nevertheless at work fulfilling His good plans.

Use the following chart to record some instances when things didn't look too good (or when you didn't understand God's plans during a hard time), and how God then turned the situation around for good. These incidents in your life are "trust and faith builders!" Refer to them when you find yourself in a hard place, struggling to trust God.

Hardship	How You Felt in the Middle of It	How God Worked it for Good in Your Life

Write out a prayer thanking God for proving Himself faithful to you.

My Prayer of Thanks for God's Faithfulness:

What will you do the next time you can't see anything good in your circumstances? Be specific.

Looking to Jesus

Millie's favorite time of the day was when she could walk to Keiths' hill to read her Bible or just to talk to Jesus. She found that she had much more patience with her students if she prayed for them, spending time talking to Jesus about their needs. At the swing one day, Millie realized that she hadn't even thought of pinching Cyril or Don in the longest time. It was strange, she couldn't remember when the impulse had stopped troubling her. Mamma's prayer had worked—Jesus was making her more patient! And the strangest thing was how it had happened. She hadn't tried to stop pinching at all. She had just tried to be like Jesus. He was changing her heart a little bit at a time. Millie made the swing fly that day, almost touching heaven with her toes.

—From *Millie's Unsettled Season*, page 208

Millie was excited! She was seeing real change in her life! Pinching her brothers, which was once a *tremendous* struggle, was now not even an issue for her. We all want to see real change in our lives. We all want to overcome weaknesses and grow in our walk with God. The key is looking to Jesus.

What are some weaknesses you'd like to overcome? Be as specific as possible, and be honest.

In the above excerpt, Millie realized that she hadn't even thought about pinching her brothers in a long time. How did she overcome this struggle?

 *Jesus* will change us as we look to Him. As we focus on Him, we receive His grace and power to overcome our weaknesses. We cannot always change ourselves nor can we always, in our own strength, overcome our weaknesses. But when we look to Jesus, He changes our heart and our behavior!

 As a modern-day pioneer for God, our focus must be on Jesus, not anything else!

Hebrews 12:2a says, "Let us fix our eyes on Jesus, the author and perfecter of our faith." Based on this passage of Scripture, who is responsible for perfecting you?

Are you trusting Jesus to perfect your faith, or are you trying to do it yourself? Write down your thoughts and give some examples.

Jesus will indeed change us when we look to Him. The first part of Hebrews 12:1 tells us that we need to "throw off everything that hinders and the sin that so easily entangles." It goes on to encourage us to "run with perseverance the race marked out for us." Those hindrances and sins in our life block us from clearly seeing the Lord, which in turn blocks us from real change and growth.

What are the things that hinder you? Are you aware of any sins that easily entangle you?

 **We can be so absorbed in our own weaknesses or disappointing circumstances that we become distracted in our "race" — distracted to the point that we look away from Jesus. But a pioneer for God cannot let distractions keep her from God!**

Let's read about a famous disciple who let distractions take his focus off of Jesus:

Immediately Jesus made the disciples get into the boat and go on ahead of him to the other side, while he dismissed the crowd. After he had dismissed them, he went up on a mountainside by himself to pray. When evening came, he was there alone, but the boat was already a considerable distance from land, buffeted by the waves because the wind was against it.

During the fourth watch of the night Jesus went out to them, walking on the lake. When the disciples saw him walking on the lake, they were terrified. "It's a ghost," they said, and cried out in fear.

But Jesus immediately said to them: "Take courage! It is I. Don't be afraid."

"Lord, if it's you, " Peter replied, "tell me to come to you on the water."

"Come," he said.

Then Peter got down out of the boat, walked on the water and came toward Jesus. But when he saw the wind, he was afraid and, beginning to sink, cried out, "Lord, save me!"

Immediately Jesus reached out his hand and caught him. "You of little faith," he said, "why did you doubt?"

And when they climbed into the boat, the wind died down. Then those who were in the boat worshiped him, saying, "Truly you are the Son of God."

— Matthew 14:22–33

What happened when Peter took his eyes off of Jesus?

Peter became focused on the troubling circumstances surrounding him—the wild wind and pounding waves. His own fears caused him to look away from Jesus, distracting him away from an incredible moment with the Lord!

As we've read, Hebrews 12:1–2 compares life to a race. What happens if, while running a race, you turn around to look at the other racers behind you? More than likely you would break your stride and possibly trip and fall, losing your place in the race.

A pioneer for God runs the race with intensity, straining with every fiber of her being to reach the goal, which is Jesus at the finish line waiting with your reward!

The apostle Paul said, "Not that I have already obtained all this, or have already been made perfect, but I press on to take hold of that for which Christ Jesus took hold of me. Brothers, I do not consider myself yet to have taken hold of it. But one thing I do: Forgetting what is behind and straining toward what is ahead, I press on toward the goal to win the prize for which God has called me heavenward in Christ Jesus" (Philippians 3:12–14).

What did Paul do with his past?

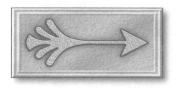

Do not let the past keep you from moving forward.

Is there something in your past hindering you? If so, what is it and in what ways does it hinder you?

Ask the Holy Spirit to reveal if something from your past is stopping you from straining toward the prize. You may want to speak with an adult to pray and talk about your past. God wants you to be free from unforgiveness or any other hindrance so that you can run the race with strength!

Look back over this chapter. Ask the Holy Spirit to show you the most important things He wants you to remember. Put a star beside those truths and, in your own words, summarize below what He showed you.

Rewrite your thoughts as a prayer, asking God to help you grow and apply the truths He's taught you throughout the chapter.

Write out the memory verse for this chapter, Romans 8:28:

Write out the memory verse for our entire study, Proverbs 3:5–6:

CHAPTER

Seeing with Eyes of Faith

Seeing with Eyes of Faith

by heart

*N*ow faith is being sure of what we hope for and certain of what we do not see.
— HEBREWS 11:1

Faith Versus Feelings

*M*illie's eyes misted with emotion. *I am not going to start that again!* She pulled her knees up and rested her chin on them.

"Trust in the Lord with all your heart and lean not on your own understanding. In all your ways acknowledge him, and he will make your paths straight." Could it have been only months since her mother had given her that verse? That trusty chair in the washroom seemed a hundred years in the past. It hadn't let her fall. *But I feel like I'm falling, God. I feel like I'm tumbling, tumbling down, and I just haven't hit the ground yet.* That was just it. She hadn't hit the ground. Maybe she wasn't falling at all.

Mamma has lost a lot more than I have, and she is still trusting God. Jesus, I want to trust You like that. I want to know You like that. But I don't know how yet. Millie sat up and straightened her shoulders. *I'm going to try to be like Mamma while I learn.*

Suddenly the Scripture from the night in the hotel came back into her mind, sharp and clear: *"I will give you the treasures of darkness, riches stored in secret places, so that you may know that I am the Lord, the God of Israel, who summons you by name."*

"Jesus," Millie prayed, "are You going to show me the treasures hidden in Pleasant Plains?"

— From *Millie's Unsettled Season*, page 133

*M*illie experienced *many* different feelings and emotions when her world was turned upside down with a move to Pleasant Plains. Her feelings often confused her, because what she felt was different from what God's Word promised. Millie had to learn to allow

her *faith* to influence her thoughts and behaviors more than her *feelings*, and this is no easy task for a young girl!

But God wanted Millie's faith to grow stronger, and He wants your faith to grow stronger too. One thing that can really hinder a growing faith in Christ is when our feelings and emotions get out of hand and influence our thoughts and behaviors.

In the above passage, we can see how Millie knew her emotions (feelings) were trying to get the best of her. "Millie's eyes misted with emotion. *I am not going to start that again!* She pulled her knees up and rested her chin on them." Millie immediately recognized that her emotions were affecting her faith, making her doubt God's good plan for her and her family.

What negative feelings do you most commonly experience? Check any boxes that apply:

❑ fear   ❑ selfishness   ❑ confusion   ❑ other_____

❑ sadness   ❑ jealousy   ❑ frustration   ❑ other_____

❑ anger   ❑ boredom   ❑ hatred   ❑ other_____

What circumstances provoke those feelings in you? For instance, friendship quarrels may cause you to feel jealousy and sadness. A conflict with your parents or siblings may cause you to feel frustrated and angry. Write your thoughts below:

Pick one feeling from the ones you checked above (choose a feeling that you experience more than the others) and explain how this feeling controls the way you think and behave.

Example:

I feel — Selfishness.

I think — I have to have my own way or I won't be happy.

I behave — with a bad attitude; like a spoiled child; in a self-centered way, like I'm better than others.

Your response:

I feel — _____

I think — _____

I behave — _____

How is your behavior and thinking in opposition to how God wants you to live?

As believers, we must learn to respond to life's situations with faith and not feelings.

Second Corinthians 5:7 says we are to "walk by faith, not by sight." Walking by faith means we choose to believe and act according to what God says. Walking by sight means we choose to believe and act according to what we see or feel in our natural world around us.

Hebrews 4:12 instructs us that the Word of God is living, active, and as sharp as a double-edged sword which will divide soul and spirit, and judges the thoughts and attitudes of the heart. God's Word will help us sort out His truth from the emotions that originate in our souls (our soul is the thoughts in our minds, the choices we make with our will, and the emotions we feel).

If your emotions or attitudes seem inappropriate or in turmoil, check your thoughts. Chances are that somewhere, you've chosen to believe what you see or feel rather than what God has spoken.

God has given us Philippians 4:8 to use as an "attitude check." Look it up in your Bible and write it out here:

Second Corinthians 10:5 instructs us to take every thought captive and make it obey Christ. Any thought that does not line up with Philippians 4:8 must be stopped or changed, and we should choose instead to submit to God's truth and align our thoughts with His Word. This is called an "attitude adjustment." Controlling your thought life will require some discipline on your part. You may find it a constant battle at first to stop those disobedient and unrestrained thoughts, but persevere at it. It takes a while to break old thought patterns. Soon you will find your thoughts will become more trained to become Christlike.

 **Disciplining your thoughts and making them obedient to Christ will make them stronger than your emotions. This will enable you to behave the way you want regardless of how you feel. Philippians 4:8 should be the standard for your thought life.**

In general, how do you think your thoughts line up with Philippians 4:8?

What negative or wrong thought patterns do you wrestle with the most? (Hint: look back at the exercise where you described your feelings, thoughts, and behaviors.)

Now, let's take those feelings and thoughts we were working with earlier, and let's apply the principle we've learned in 2 Corinthians 10:5 and Philippians 4:8. You are going to identify the wrong thoughts and feelings by comparing them to Philippians 4:8. If they don't pass the test, you are going to "arrest" them, and replace them with a spiritual truth from God's Word.

Take the same feeling you listed above and write down how responding in faith can help you overcome your feelings. Let's take God's sword and "arrest" those disobedient thoughts.

Example:

Feeling — Selfishness

Thoughts of Faith — Generosity; giving to others.

New Response — I don't have to be selfish because I can trust in faith that God blesses those who have generous hearts.

God's Word says — "Freely you have received, freely give." (Matthew 10:8)

Your Response:

Feeling — _____

Thoughts of Faith — _____

New Response — I don't have to be _____ because I can trust in faith that

_____

God's Word says — _____

What feelings and responses of faith will you focus on this week?

In our opening excerpt, Millie found herself struggling with her emotions. She could only see the hardships in front of her, and this got in the way of her being able to see through eyes of faith. She had to combat her feelings with faith in God. She pondered Proverbs 3:5–6 in her heart and knew she had to trust Jesus and not let her heart be troubled.

Write out our memory verse for this chapter, Hebrews 11:1.

Faith is hoping in the unseen world of God's Kingdom that includes His truth, promises, and principles. Allowing our emotions to control us is putting our faith in the "seen" physical world around us. Our hope of overcoming our feelings must be rooted in Jesus Christ. Trusting in Him gives us hope of a future and destiny. Put your hope in the eternal Kingdom of God that will never pass away. In Philippians 4:13 we are given the assurance that we can do everything when God gives us the strength. Look to God for the strength to overcome your feelings and step out in faith!

Grasshopper or Eagle?

> "Would you like to take the maps to school with you today, to show your friends?"
>
> "Oh, Aunty," Millie's eyes filled with tears again. "That's the worst part, the part I can't bear—no more school for me. There's too much sewing and packing to do between now and when we leave. But what's worse is that out on the frontier, there won't be school for me either—at least not like I have with Mr. Martin."
>
> "No school?" Aunt Wealthy was speechless for a full minute. She brushed a tear from Millie's face. "You will still have books, and your father and mother—both educated people—will help you, and who knows but what you may end up with a better education than school can provide. I've found that the knowledge I've gained by my own efforts is often the most useful. Your skill with a needle and thread wasn't learned in school. You are a great help and comfort to your mother because of it."
>
> —From *Millie's Unsettled Season*, page 8

Remember when Millie got the news that they were really moving to Pleasant Plains? She had a hard time seeing any good in the whole situation. Instead, Millie saw only what she would be missing. She could only see the negative side of things, like the fact that she would not have her school or Mr. Martin to teach her.

To see with eyes of faith (and to overcome our emotions), we need to try and look at the positive in our circumstances. Aunt Wealthy was able to see beyond Millie's heartache of leaving her home, friends, and school. Aunt Wealthy knew it would be hard for Millie, and Wealthy didn't try to negate Millie's feelings. But Aunt Wealthy helped Millie see beyond the heartache. Aunt Wealthy looked for the good in Millie's situation.

Do you see through eyes of faith? Read the following story taken from Numbers 13:1–2; 17–20; and 26–33, and answer the questions that follow.

> The LORD said to Moses, "Send some men to explore the land of Canaan, which I am giving to the Israelites." . . . When Moses sent them to explore Canaan, he said, "Go up through the Negev and on into the hill country. See what the land is like and whether the people who live there are strong or weak, few or many. What kind of land do they live in? Is it good or bad? What kind of towns do they live in? Are they unwalled or fortified? How is the soil? Is it fertile or poor? Are there trees on it or not? Do your best

EING WITH EYES OF FAITH

to bring back some of the fruit of the land." (It was the season for the first ripe grapes.) . . .

They came back to Moses and Aaron and the whole Israelite community at Kadesh in the Desert of Paran. There they reported to them and to the whole assembly and showed them the fruit of the land. They gave Moses this account: "We went into the land to which you sent us, and it does flow with milk and honey! Here is its fruit. But the people who live there are powerful, and the cities are fortified and very large. We even saw descendants of Anak there. The Amalekites live in the Negev; the Hittites, Jebusites and Amorites live in the hill country; and the Canaanites live near the sea and along the Jordan."

Then Caleb silenced the people before Moses and said, "We should go up and take possession of the land, for we can certainly do it." But the men who had gone up with him said, "We can't attack those people; they are stronger than we are." And they spread among the Israelites a bad report about the land they had explored. They said, "The land we explored devours those living in it. All the people we saw there are of great size. We saw the Nephilim there (the descendants of Anak come from the Nephilim). We seemed like grasshoppers in our own eyes, and we looked the same to them."

—Numbers 13:17–20, 26–33

List seven things Moses wanted the men to find out in Canaan:

1)   What is the land like: good or bad?

2)

3)

4)

5)

6)

7)

What was Joshua and Caleb's report about the land?

What did the other men report to Moses?

If Joshua and Caleb considered all the same things that the other men saw, why was their conclusion different? Because Joshua and Caleb saw with eyes of faith. They chose to believe what God promised them. Joshua and Caleb saw the powerful men living in the land, but were not intimidated by them as the other spies were. Joshua and Caleb put their trust in God and His Word to them — that He would give them the land: "The LORD said to Moses, 'Send some men to explore the land of Canaan, which I am giving to the Israelites'"(Numbers 13:1–2).

Write out our Scripture memory verse, Proverbs 3:5–6.

Joshua and Caleb saw one thing — the strength and size of the people of Canaan — but they believed something different: that God would enable them to take the land. Remember, we walk by <u>faith</u>, not by <u>sight</u>. (See 2 Corinthians 5:7) They trusted God and relied on God's understanding, not their own. That's why they were able to say with confidence, "We should go up and take possession of the land, for we can certainly do it."

Because Joshua and Caleb believed God, they were able to have the exalted viewpoint of an eagle. Since they were looking to Jesus through eyes of faith and not at their circumstances (the giants of the land), God was bigger to them than these giants of Canaan. They became <u>convinced</u> that what God said was true, not what their eyes were telling them. This is the faith spoken of in your chapter memory verse, Hebrews 11:1. Look it up and write it out.

The other scouts, through their unbelief, had the viewpoint of a grasshopper. They were choosing to focus on their human weaknesses and the power of the enemy. This is not faith—it is walking by sight. They did not choose to believe that God would be faithful to do what He said. As we learned earlier, our negative, unbelieving attitudes can infect others. The rest of the Israelites became frightened because of this negative report, and also chose not to believe.

The really sad part of the story is seen in Numbers 13. Because the Israelites did not believe, they could not possess this wonderful land promised to them. Instead, they had to wander for 40 years in the wilderness until a new generation was raised up that believed God. Only Joshua and Caleb were able to obtain the promise.

 **Two people can view the very same situation differently. We can miss the promises and good plans that God has for us if we choose to respond in unbelief.**

Look closely at your life. Are you a grasshopper or an eagle?

Millie was learning to trust God in her own situation. She had giants to face: the possibility of no school or friends and an unknown place to live in. Aunt Wealthy was teaching Millie to see through eyes of faith, looking for the good, and keeping her eyes on Jesus. God was transforming Millie: from seeing her circumstances as a grasshopper to seeing them as an eagle.

What circumstance are you facing right now, where you are "seeing as a grasshopper instead of seeing as an eagle"?

Now, go back to God's Word and find a promise you can believe for this circumstance. Look for the list of promises in the next lesson if you need help.

Relying on the Promises

> *W*hat are we going to do without Celestia Ann, Lord? wondered Millie. . . .
>
> "Why so serious, my dear?" Aunt Wealthy asked, taking Millie's hand. "Didn't you think it was a delightful wedding?"
>
> "Yes," Millie said, "it was wonderful. I was hoping that I can be as much of a help to Mamma as Celestia Ann was."
>
> Aunt Wealthy squeezed her hand. "We will all have to do a little more, but I believe Philippians 4:13, that we can do everything through Christ Jesus who gives us strength," she said, sharing a familiar Bible verse.
>
> —From *Millie's Courageous Days*, pages 105–106

Have you ever felt some doubt or uncertainty about your own abilities, like Millie did in this excerpt? Millie felt uncertain that she'd be able to help her Mamma as much as Celestia Ann had. But when we have doubts and uncertainties we can turn to God's promises, like Aunt Wealthy did.

 **Whether in good times or bad, hard or easy, we need to cling to the promises of God's Word.**

In lesson four of chapter two we studied about the sovereignty of God—that even though God tends to the matters of the universe, He holds you close to His heart! He cares about what's going on in your life and He yearns for a personal relationship with you!

The Lord wants us to live our lives with strong faith in Him. To do this we must know the powerful promises of God's Word and trust that what God says is true. Knowing God's promises and trusting in them equip us to face any doubt, hardship, or challenge with godly confidence.

 **Sometimes God asks us to trust Him for what looks impossible to us, but do not lean on your own understanding of what "impossible" means. (Proverbs 3:5–6) "Nothing is impossible to God." (Matthew 19:26)**

Let's look and see how a great pioneer of faith, Abraham, trusted the promises of God. When God promised Abraham a son, Abraham and his wife, Sarah, were well past the age of childbearing. But God promised him a son, and that through the son Abraham would raise up descendants as numerous as the stars in the sky, making Abraham a "father of many nations."

> Therefore, the promise comes by faith, so that it may be by grace and may be guaranteed to all Abraham's offspring—not only to those who are of the law but also to those who are of the faith of Abraham. He is the father of us all. As it is written: "I have made you a father of many nations." He is our father in the sight of God, in whom he believed—the God who gives life to the dead and calls things that are not as though they were. Against all hope, Abraham believed and so became the father of many nations, just as it had been said to him, "So shall your offspring be." Without weakening in his faith, he faced the fact that his body was as good as dead. Yet he did not waver through unbelief regarding the promise of God, but was strengthened in his faith and gave glory to God, being fully persuaded that God had power to do what he had promised. This is why "it was credited to him as righteousness." The words "it was credited to him" were written not for him alone, but also for us, to whom God will credit righteousness—for us who believe in him who raised Jesus our LORD from the dead. He was delivered over to death for our sins and was raised to life for our justification.
>
> —Romans 4:16–25

In the passage above,

1)   Circle the word *believe* every time you see it.

2)   Underline the word *promise* every time you see it.

3)   Draw a box around the word *faith* every time you see it.

Fill in the blank:

The promise comes by _____.

Abraham could hope because he_____God could do what He

promised.

Are you facing a situation where you feel hopeless? Describe it below:

Abraham was fully _____ that God had the _____

to do what He _____. (Romans 4:21)

Promises, promises. You've heard that expression before, but do you realize how many promises God has made that apply to us? Read through the following list:

Deuteronomy 31:8 — The LORD himself goes before you and will be with you; he will never leave you nor forsake you. Do not be afraid; do not be discouraged.

Isaiah 66:13 — As a mother comforts her child, so will I comfort you.

1 John 1:9 — If we confess our sins, he is faithful and just and will forgive us our sins and purify us from all unrighteousness.

Philippians 4:6–7 — Do not be anxious about anything, but in everything, by prayer and petition, with thanksgiving, present your requests to God. And the peace of God, which transcends all understanding, will guard your hearts and your minds in Christ Jesus.

Philippians 1:6 — Being confident of this, that he who began a good work in you will carry it on to completion until the day of Christ Jesus.

Philippians 4:19 — And my God will meet all your needs according to his glorious riches in Christ Jesus.

Philippians 4:13 — I can do everything through him who gives me strength.

Romans 10:9 — If you confess with your mouth, "Jesus is LORD," and believe in your heart that God raised him from the dead, you will be saved.

Jude 1:24 — To him who is able to keep you from falling and to present you before his glorious presence without fault and with great joy….

Romans 8:28 — And we know that in all things God works for the good of those who love him, who have been called according to his purpose.

Romans 8:38-39 — For I am convinced that neither death nor life, neither angels nor demons, neither the present nor the future, nor any powers, neither height nor depth, nor anything else in all creation, will be able to separate us from the love of God that is in Christ Jesus our LORD.

Isaiah 41:13 — For I am the LORD, your God, who takes hold of your right hand and says to you, Do not fear; I will help you.

Psalm 27:1 — The LORD is my light and my salvation—whom shall I fear? The LORD is the stronghold of my life— of whom shall I be afraid?

Find a promise on the list that can help you with your struggles, and fill in the chart.

My Struggle	Scripture Verse	God's Promise to me is . . .

Are *you* fully persuaded that God has the power to do what He promises? Yes or No? What is our response to God which "credits" or gives us righteousness through the death and resurrection of Jesus? (Romans 4:24)

It's all about believing (faith). We receive salvation through Jesus by believing, and we receive the promises of God in His Word by believing.

Even Millie had to learn to believe God's promises. In the midst of her feelings of inadequacy she had to choose to believe the promise that God had given her in Philippians 4:13.

> Jeremiah 32:17 — Ah, Sovereign LORD, you have made the heavens and the earth by your great power and outstretched arm. Nothing is too hard for you.

It's a Choice!

*R*u returned just before sunset, stopping Millie in the yard and taking the bucket of water from her hand. "No one can help us," he said. "No one can come. They all have sick ones of their own to mind—and I couldn't find the Lords. What am I going to tell Mamma, Millie? She's all done in from nursing the sick ones."

Marcia must have read the news on his face when he came in the door. "God is still with us," she said, "and He is still in control. Let's move all the children to the sitting room. It will be easier to care for them there. I'll take care of Pappa myself."

Why not move Pappa, too? Millie thought, suddenly chilled. *Is he too ill? Or even . . .* she couldn't complete the thought, it was too terrible. And she didn't dare ask in front of the children. She helped move the small patients one by one onto cots and mats in the sitting room. She sighed with relief when Marcia carried a pitcher of water up to Stuart's room. *He's alive. Mamma wouldn't carry water up if he weren't.*

"Millie, will you bathe Cyril's face with a cool cloth, while I bathe Don's? And Adah, bring your Bible. You can read to us."

Adah brought her Bible from her room. "Which part, Mamma?"

> "I've always loved Psalm 100," Marcia said. "I would like to hear it now."
>
> " 'Shout for joy to the Lord, all the earth'," Adah began. " 'Worship the Lord with gladness; come before him with joyful songs. Know that the Lord is God. It is he who made us, and we are his; we are his people, the sheep of his pasture.'"
>
> Cyril tossed and turned beneath the cool cloth as Adah's voice went on. Marcia joined in the last verse. " 'For the Lord is good and his love endures forever; his faithfulness continues through all generations.' "
>
> — From *Millie's Courageous Days*, pages 214–215

Marcia had nothing but God's promises to lean on. She had to trust in God's sovereignty for herself and her family. If Marcia only looked at the situation through her human eyes, what would she have seen? The situation would have looked hopeless! All the odds seemed to be against her and her family. But instead, Marcia *chose* to put her trust in God and lean on His understanding of their circumstances, not her own. She listened to the promises found in Psalm 100 and believed that God was good and actively working in her distressing situation.

Look up Psalm 100 and answer the following questions:

1. Who made you?

2. How long does God's love endure?

3. Who does God promise to be faithful to?

Psalm 100 is actually a psalm for giving thanks! That's the psalm Marcia picked in the midst of a very hard time for the whole family — a psalm of thanksgiving! Why do you think Psalm 100 gave Marcia great comfort?

Marcia relied on the promise that God's faithfulness would continue through all generations. She relied on the fact that her children and husband were made by God, and therefore cherished by God. Even in the midst of her own weariness, fears, and uncertainties about the situation, Marcia gave thanks to God and put her trust in Him.

When you choose to praise and give thanks to God in the midst of your trial, you will find renewed joy and strength from God to overcome.

Look up these Scriptures in your Bible and fill in the blanks with the missing words for the verses below.

Philippians 4:4 — Rejoice in the LORD _____. I will say it again: Rejoice!

Ephesians 5:19–20 — Sing and make music in your heart to the LORD, _____ giving thanks to God the Father for everything, in the name of our LORD Jesus Christ.

1 Thessalonians 5:16–17 — Be joyful _____; pray _____; give thanks in _____ circumstances, for this is God' will for you in Christ Jesus.

When are you encouraged to rejoice and give thanks?

What is the purpose and benefit of doing it?

When Paul and Silas were beaten and imprisoned, they began to pray and sing praises to God. God's power came in a violent earthquake that shook the prison, opened all the prison doors, and loosened everybody's chains! (Acts, chapter 16)

We've learned from earlier lessons that trials and hardships will come. We will feel at times like we are chained in a prison with no way out. This is the time to praise.

Praise releases the power of God into your situation. Praise lifts your faith and gets your eyes back on the One who will deliver you. God opens your prison doors when you choose through faith to praise Him.

It's a choice! We praise God because He is worthy—in spite of (regardless of) how we feel.

Millie found her mother in the room off the kitchen where the washing was done. She stood for just one moment, watching her. Millie thought she was beautiful, even in her housedress with her sleeves rolled up and her arms deep in the big washtub of soapy water. Before Pappa had lost his money, the washer woman would have done the laundry; now the family had only the help of a cook. Once upon a time, Millie and her Mamma would have had time to read books and take walks with the children. But now, Millie watched the little ones while Mamma kept house. Washing alone for eight children took half the day! The clothes had to boiled and scrubbed in the big wash bucket, wrung by hand and hung on the line. When they were dry, Millie would take them down and Mamma would iron them.

— From *Millie's Unsettled Season*, page 15

"But it doesn't make sense! Didn't He know that Mr. Arnold would embezzle Pappa's money? That we would be poor and have to move?"

"It is hard. And a little scary. But you know, daughter, you are not the only one who has memory verses. Do you want to hear mine?"

Millie nodded.

"It's Hebrews 13:5: 'Make sure that your character is free from the love of money, being content with what you have; for he himself has said, "I will never desert you, nor will I ever forsake you," so that we confidently can say, "the Lord is my helper, I will not be afraid. What will man do to me?"' If Jesus was everything to me when I had servants and wore silks, Millie mine, how could He not be everything still, even if I am a servant and wear...suds?" She blew a bubble from the tips of her fingers.

— From *Millie's Unsettled Season*, page 16

In these excerpts we see Millie struggling with feeling frustrated or disappointed with God for the sudden decline in their family's living conditions. That was an understandable reaction for a young girl to have. She is learning from her mother, Marcia, the importance of being grateful and content with what God has given. Marcia could have succumbed to grumbling or complaining about having to work hard. She could have developed a bitter, unforgiving attitude toward God, or toward Mr. Arnold for stealing their money. Instead, she chose to accept the circumstances as being a part of God's GOOD plan. This gave her the ability to be content and even thankful. Jesus truly was everything to her.

To be content, you must trust that God has arranged the circumstances of your life just the way He wants them, because He has a "good" work to accomplish through it.

You make decisions every day. You decide what clothes to wear, what you will eat for lunch, how much time you will spend on your homework. But did you know that you can make faith choices, too? You can decide to think about whatever is true, noble, right, pure, lovely, or admirable—things that are excellent or praiseworthy. You can choose to be thankful and to praise in the midst of trials and you can choose to trust God and be content with what He has given you.

Read Philippians 4:19, Hebrews 13:5–6, and Psalm 34:10. Then summarize them in the space below.

How can the promises found in these Scriptures help us choose contentment?

As you grow to love the Lord more, you will come to understand that your need for Jesus is greater than any other need you have. You learn to trust Him for all your other needs, and you will find you lack no good thing!

Paul said in Philippians 4:11–13, "I am not saying this because I am in need, for I have learned to be content whatever the circumstances. I know what it is to be in need, and I know what it is to have plenty. I have learned the secret of being content in any and every situation, whether well fed or hungry, whether living in plenty or in want. I can do everything through him who gives me strength."

What was Paul's secret for being content?

Marcia also knew Paul's secret. They both knew Jesus was with them, and that He would never forsake them. He would meet ALL their needs.

Write about a situation you are in where you are finding it hard to be content. It may be a struggle to be content with a person you have to live with, or the way you look, or anything that is bothering you.

In this lesson you learned a principle that will help you choose contentment. Describe it in your own words.

Do you remember Hebrews 11:1? Write it again here.

Persisting in Prayer

*M*illie caught the sob before it could escape her throat and covered her face with her hands. *We could all be in our graves before Aunt Wealthy even hears we are sick. What do I do? Lord, show me what to do! Why haven't You sent rain? We're desperate! Why are You allowing this to happen? Didn't You hear Mamma's prayers? Any of our prayers?*

Millie could almost hear Aunt Wealthy's voice. *"God calls us to a wild adventure, not a tea party, my dear. God has not answered our prayers yet with a yes or a no. And until He does, Millie, we just keep praying."*

"What are we going to do?" Ru repeated.

"First, we are going to pray," Millie said, getting down on her knees.

"We've been praying!" exclaimed Adah. "It isn't working."

"It is," Millie said firmly. "Just like it worked when we prayed for Fan. We just haven't seen the answer yet."

"Are you sure?" asked Ru. Millie didn't feel sure at all, but again, Aunt Wealthy's words came to her mind: *"Sometimes the way we feel has nothing to do with what is true."* "I'm sure," Millie replied.

Adah and Ru knelt beside her and took her hands.

"Lord," Millie prayed, "we need You. You said in Your Word we could call upon You in the day of trouble and that You would help us. We need Your help, desperately! Give us courage and keep us strong, and show us how to help our family. Please make them well, Jesus. You've *got* to heal them," pleaded Millie.

"And send help," Ru added. "Send help."

"Yes, Lord, send help quickly. Amen."

"Now what, Millie?" asked Ru.

"Now we do our best," she said. "Bring me some willow branches, Ru."

— From *Millie's Courageous Days*, pages 216–217

You may wonder how persisting in prayer could relate to our chapter topic, *Seeing with Eyes of Faith*. But it is in faith that we cry out to the Lord, just like Millie and the children did. Jesus said in Matthew 21:21–22, "I tell you the truth, if you have faith and do not doubt, not only can you do what was done to the fig tree, but also you can say to this mountain, 'Go throw yourself into the sea,' and it will be done. If you believe, you will receive whatever you ask for in prayer."

It's important to remember that Millie's own trust in God was growing. Millie certainly hadn't "arrived" in her faith. She still had uncertainties and doubts of her own. But she was growing. Despite her fears, she still stepped out and prayed against all the odds. Her adventure in trusting God began the day the decision was made to move to Pleasant Plains. And since that day, God was stretching and maturing Millie in her faith through circumstances just like the one in our excerpt for this lesson. God wants to stretch and grow you in your own faith as well! He desires for you to step out and pray in faith in the middle of your own doubts or fears. That's seeing through eyes of faith.

To *persist* means to continue steadfastly or often annoyingly, especially in spite of opposition. To persist in prayer means you keep on praying and you don't give up until you see the answer, even if it takes a long time.

Can you recall a time when you were filled with questions, uncertainties, or doubts and found it hard to persist in your prayers?

Why do you think it was hard to pray during that time?

As we've been studying in this chapter, our feelings can get in the way of our faith and even hinder our prayers. In the preceding excerpt, Millie herself was fighting against her feelings, but Aunt Wealthy's wise words flashed through her mind: *Sometimes the way we feel has nothing to do with what is true.* Aunt Wealthy taught Millie to be persistent in her prayers—to keep praying in every situation until God answered—*regardless of feelings*. It's not always easy to rise above our feelings and emotions and commit to prayer, but it is possible!

Write out our memory verse for this chapter, Hebrews 11:1:

It takes faith to pray. We can pray with persistence and confidence if we are convinced that God hears and answers our prayers. (Psalm 65:2)

Romans 8:26 — In the same way, the Spirit helps us in our weakness. We do not know what we ought to pray for, but the Spirit himself intercedes for us with groans that words cannot express.

The Holy Spirit will help you with prayer. He will tell you what to pray for and enable you to pray.

 **Learn to pray *with* the Holy Spirit, trusting and believing Him to help you in your weakness and inability. Be a young woman of powerful, persistent prayer!**

The Word tells us to pray always, devoting ourselves to prayer. Obviously prayer is such a vital part of our Christian walk! Look up the following verses and fill in the missing words.

1) 1 Thessalonians 5:16–18

Be _____ always; pray _____; give _____ in all circumstances, for this is God's _____ for you in Christ Jesus.

2) Colossians 4:2

Devote yourself to _____, being _____ and _____.

3) James 5:17–18

Elijah was a man just like us. He prayed _____ that it would not rain, and it did not rain on the land for three and a half years. Again he _____, and the heavens gave rain, and the earth produced its crops.

God has given us such a privilege through prayer to become a partner with Him in seeing His purposes accomplished on the earth.

Becoming a young woman committed to prayer will transform your life and the lives of others! The more you pray and talk with God, the more you will know Him and trust Him in your adventures.

Do you have a prayer request that you can commit to persistent prayer? Write the need below and commit to pray earnestly until God answers!

As you step out and become a prayer warrior, God will begin to reveal fruit from your persistent prayers. Millie saw fruit from her own prayers. Fan recovered from her fall, God brought new friends into Millie's life, and the Lord healed the Keiths from the ague sickness. Millie kept a journal of her prayers, people she was praying for, and other prayer requests and how God answered them. If you don't have a prayer journal, consider starting one. You will be encouraged in your growth to see God moving in your life and in the lives of others because of your faithful prayers!

Look back over this chapter. Ask the Holy Spirit to show you the most important things He wants you to remember. Put a star beside those truths and, in your own words, summarize below what He showed you.

Rewrite your thoughts as a prayer, asking God to help you grow and apply the truths He's taught you throughout the chapter.

Write out the memory verse for this chapter, Hebrews 11:1:

Write out the memory verse for our entire study, Proverbs 3:5–6:

CHAPTER

7

Trusting God in Relationships

Lesson 1
The Fire of Conflict

Lesson 2
Courage to Love

Lesson 3
Seeing Through the Eyes of Jesus

Lesson 4
Trusting God for Others' Salvation

Lesson 5
Looking Back on the Adventure

Trusting God in Relationships

by heart

*B*ut he said to me, "My grace is sufficient for you, for my power is made perfect in weakness." Therefore I will boast all the more gladly about my weaknesses, so that Christ's power may rest on me. That is why, for Christ's sake, I delight in weaknesses, in insults, in hardships, in persecutions, in difficulties. For when I am weak, then I am strong.
—2 CORINTHIANS 12:9–10

The Fire of Conflict

*M*illie began to feel very uncomfortable, and Lucilla noticed at once. "Oh, Millie," she said. "I apologize! How rude of us. You weren't at the party, and know nothing of these people!"

"I'm sure Millie enjoys an intrigue as much as the rest of us," Helen said. "I love Emma's tales!"

Millie bit her lip. If she were in Lansdale, she would have quoted Pappa: "Repeating second-hand knowledge is hearsay in the courts of man, and gossip in the courts of heaven. I don't want to be guilty of either!" She wasn't in Lansdale with her friends, though. She was an invited guest in a new place. But wasn't right right and wrong wrong no matter where you were? And God's Word was very clear about gossip.

"I think…" Millie began, but at that moment Mrs. Chetwood came out to offer the sandwiches and lemonade she had prepared. She encouraged the girls to start on the verse at hand as soon as they were finished eating. Millie was relieved, but a little ashamed of herself for not finishing her sentence.
—From *Millie's Unsettled Season*, pages 162–163

*I*n the passage above we see Millie's first interaction with the girls of Pleasant Plains. When they began to gossip, she immediately felt uncomfortable. In her *heart* Millie knew that gossip was against God's Word. And now in her *mind* a conflict began. Should she speak the truth and risk being rejected by the girls, or should she just keep quiet and try to blend in, despite her discomfort? Millie first met with an internal conflict. She wrestled with the dilemma of either speaking what is right or shrinking back from fear of rejection. She was unsure what move to make.

Have you ever found yourself in a situation when you felt convicted to speak out, but were a bit unsure about doing it? Describe it below:

Millie didn't speak up about the gossip issue, but God brought another opportunity for Millie to speak out when the Bible study began. Millie took a chance and bravely spoke up to share God's truths and clarify the message of the Scripture that the girls were studying. Millie was aware that the girls were listening, but she wasn't absolutely sure they would agree with her. As it turned out, the girls didn't agree with her and they were very offended. It seemed like a disaster.

*C*laudina stood up, barely hiding her embarrassment. "Girls, I have to say that today's Bible study was of little value. At the very least, we should stay focused on the Scripture at hand, which was, as I recall, about the important difference between outward appearances and what's in one's heart!"

Lu and Helen stared first at Claudina and then at Millie.

"What did I say?" Lu asked. "I am sorry if I spoke out of turn or offended anyone here. Though I do think I have a right to my opinion." She and Helen both stood to leave. Everyone said their good-byes, but Millie could barely speak. Her tears were too near falling.

When the other girls had left, she turned to Claudina.

"I am so sorry," she said. "It was a perfectly lovely afternoon and I spoiled it."

"I will admit we have never had a Bible study quite like that before," Claudina said. "But I don't think you said anything wrong. How can you study the Bible and not speak the truth? Besides, I know Helen and Lu. They will have forgotten about it by tomorrow." She walked Millie to the door.

"I want to apologize to you, Millie," she said. "I knew you were right, and I didn't stand up for you. I am so envious of your courage!"

"I was afraid to truly speak my mind," Millie confessed. "If my temper hadn't flared, I might not have. My friends in Lansdale would have chided me for that."

—From *Millie's Unsettled Season*, pages 166–167

Can you imagine how Millie must have felt walking out of the Bible study? She must have wondered if she would ever fit in with the girls of Pleasant Plains. After all, the first encounter she had with them turned into a conflict of ideas and morals. What a first impression she made! Her courage definitely made a beautiful impression on God's heart (He loves it when we stand up for His truths!), and it made a lasting impression on Claudina for God's glory. Even if Lu and Helen left the Bible study offended, God still used Millie's boldness in their lives.

Relationships are always a challenge and we need to trust God with our relationships, especially when we run into a conflict or disagreement.

Disagreements between Christians are certainly not uncommon. For example, in Acts 15 even the apostle Paul and Barnabas disagreed and parted ways. But in the end God was able to bring forth His will. God allows these experiences and can use them for good!

Can you recall a time when your involvement in a conflict or argument had positive benefits in the end?

As Christians, we do not need to fear or shrink back from conflict. God can use conflicts for our good. He also uses them to accomplish His plans.

Read the following verses:

"I will turn my hand against you; I will thoroughly purge away your dross and remove all your impurities." (Isaiah 1:25)

"But who can endure the day of his coming? Who can stand when he appears? For he will be like a refiner's fire or a launderer's soap. He will sit as a refiner and purifier of silver." (Malachi 3:2–3)

"For you, O God, tested us; you refined us like silver." (Psalm 66:10)

 **Conflicts are opportunities to grow more like Jesus. God uses them to refine you.**

God will act as a heavenly refiner or silversmith in our lives. The dross represents our sinful nature and the silver is God's nature. The heat of the blacksmith's fire causes the impurities or dross to be separated from the metal so that what remains is fine, precious silver. God will allow the "fire" of conflict to have the same effect on our lives; a divine purging takes place where the sin nature is removed so that the precious life of Christ can come forth.

This process can be painful and cause us to feel anxious and vulnerable. From our excerpt we see that Millie did her best to juggle speaking out the truth while trying to remain kind and gracious. But sometimes our emotions rise up and we might say something that we later regret. We feel vulnerable and weak, especially when we are doing our best to express our convictions and the other person is rejecting us.

Think of a time when you had an argument in a relationship. How did it make you feel?

Consider the following verses:

Psalm 103:13–14 —
"As a father has compassion on his children, so the LORD has compassion on those who fear him; for he knows how we are formed, he remembers that we are dust."

Hebrews 4:14–16 —
"Therefore, since we have a great high priest who has gone through the heavens, Jesus the Son of God, let us hold firmly to the faith we profess. For we do not have a high priest who is unable to sympathize with our weaknesses, but we have one who has been tempted in every way, just as we are—yet was without sin. Let us then approach the throne of grace with confidence, so that we may receive mercy and find grace to help us in our time of need."

 **You can turn to God with your feelings of anxiety and vulnerability because He understands and has compassion on you. He is aware of and sympathetic toward your human weaknesses.**

God knows your heart, and He knows when your intentions are pure and noble, even if your words come out wrong. As humans, we are imperfect, and God knows this and has compassion on us. There will be dross in our lives and in our actions, even when we mean well.

Look again at your memory verse, 2 Corinthians 12:9–10:

> But he said to me, "My grace is sufficient for you, for my power is made perfect in weakness." Therefore I will boast all the more gladly about my weaknesses, so that Christ's power may rest on me. That is why, for Christ's sake, I delight in weaknesses, in insults, in hardships, in persecutions, in difficulties. For when I am weak, then I am strong."

 **We can trust the Lord for the promise that in our moments of weakness, His grace will be sufficient for us and His power will rest on us. Our weaknesses give God the opportunity to display His power.**

 **Remember in the midst of conflicts that we are called to be peacemakers.**

Hebrews 12:14 says, "Make every effort to live in peace with all men and to be holy; without holiness no one will see the Lord." Make sure you are equally concerned about understanding the other person as much as wanting to be understood. James 1:19-20 instructs us to be quick to listen, slow to speak, and slow to become angry. Anger will get the better of you sometimes. When the heat of the moment is over, a peacemaker is quick to repent, quick to forgive, and quick to make amends.

Sometimes a conflict will arise in your life because you had to speak truth and suffer rejection as a consequence. If you are troubled over a conflict in a relationship, remember that God is in the midst of it. He sees your heart. If someone comes against you because of speaking out for righteousness, consider it as participating in the suffering of Christ.

> Dear friends, do not be surprised at the painful trial you are suffering, as though something strange were happening to you. But rejoice that you participate in the sufferings of Christ, so that you may be overjoyed when his glory is revealed. If you are insulted because of the name of Christ, you are blessed, for the Spirit of glory and of God rests on you. . . . So then, those who suffer according to God's will should commit themselves to their faithful Creator and continue to do good. (1 Peter 4:12–14, 19)

How can this verse encourage you when you are rejected for standing on the truth of God's Word?

How can you trust God more with conflicts in your relationships? Explain.

Courage to Love

At dinner, pussy willows in a vase presided over the excellent meal prepared by Celestia Ann and Aunt Wealthy. Aunt Wealthy had cleaned Reverend Lord's shoe for him, and with the exception of the mud on his pants he was as good as new. The conversation turned to the sermon, which had been on the topic of forgiveness.

"Surely you can't mean that Jesus would have us be cowardly?" Nicholas inquired.

"No," Reverend Lord replied. "It seems to me that it takes more courage not to strike back, especially if one is strong. Think of what courage Jesus had, to take a beating and to be crucified, when at any moment He could have ended it all with a word. The point was, the stronger had mercy on the weaker. He had nothing but love in His heart. And sometimes it takes courage to love."

The discussion went on, sometimes quite vigorously, but Millie's mind went back to the Christmas Eve service, and the expression on her mother's face when she was speaking to Damaris. The stronger had mercy on the weaker. *I don't think I can do that,* Millie admitted silently to the Lord. *Damaris Drybread is the one person on earth I don't think I can ever love!*

—From *Millie's Courageous Days*, page 77

Have you ever felt that way about someone? We all have people like Damaris Drybread in our lives at one time or another. People we find hard to love. Millie was no different. It seemed that each time Millie found herself in a conversation with Damaris, things took a swift turn for the worse. Let's face it, Damaris was hard to like, let alone love!

It would be easy to sail through life and avoid those difficult people, wouldn't it? Perhaps you can even name a few people who you wouldn't mind never having to deal with again. But that's the easy way out, and we know by now that God calls us to something different—a better way!

 **God calls us to love. Sometimes it takes courage to love, but God will give you courage if you ask for it.**

Did you ever think you would need courage to actually love someone? Reverend Lord made a great point when he described the strength and courage Jesus had when He was beaten and crucified. Jesus *loved* the very people who were mocking and torturing Him.

In our last chapter we discussed how God gives us choices, and we in fact make many little choices each day—choices that can help us mature and grow in our faith. One of the most important choices we can make is to love.

Look up Mark 12:29–31, the greatest commandment, and complete the missing words in the verses below.

"The most _____ one," answered Jesus, "is this: 'Hear, O Israel, the LORD our God, the LORD is one. Love the LORD your _____ with all your _____ and with all your _____ and with all your _____ and with all your _____.' The second is this: 'Love your _____ as _____.' There is no commandment _____ than these."

Who do you suppose you should consider as your *neighbor*?

Damaris was a neighbor to the Keiths. She might not have lived right next door to them, like the Lightcaps did, but Damaris was a person God brought into their lives. Your neighbor could be an acquaintance at school or church. It doesn't have to be limited to people who live on your street. God wants us to love the people around us—the people He brings across our paths. Are you up to the challenge?

Can you think of someone who you need to have the courage to love? It's not an easy thing to do. You might even feel like you're too weak to love this person the way God wants you to. Millie even confessed, *"Damaris Drybread is the one person on earth I don't think I can ever love!"*

Don't despair! There's great news! Complete our memory verse for this chapter, 2 Corinthians 12:9–10.

But he said to me, "My _____ is sufficient for you, for my power is made perfect

in _____." Therefore I will boast all the more gladly about my _____,

so that Christ's _____ may rest on me. That is why, for Christ's sake, I delight

in _____, in insults, in hardships, in persecutions, in _____. For when

I am _____, then I am _____.

Now make a list of the "Damarises" in your life. One at a time, pray and ask the Lord to help you be willing to love them.

Take courage in knowing that God will give you the grace to love — His power will be made perfect in your weaknesses!

Stuart took Millie's Bible from the stand by her bed. "Being in love, the kind of love that will last a lifetime, starts right here, in 1 Corinthians 13:4. 'Love is patient, love is kind. It does not envy, it does not boast, it is not proud. It is not rude, it is not self-seeking, it is not easily angered, it keeps no record of wrongs. Love does not delight in evil but rejoices with the truth. It always protects, always trusts, always hopes, always perseveres. Love never fails.' If your feelings and your actions cannot stand up to these verses, then how could you be in love?"

"But Pappa, surely those verses are for all Christians. Isn't Paul saying that we should love everyone that way?"

"Yes, he is," Stuart laughed. "Practice it with all your might. You can start out practicing on your friends and family, but if you really want to see what God can do, practice on your enemies. It takes a lot of work—and courage, too. But keep at it. And when it is time for you to fall in love, God will add something special and wonderful. Now, is that enough of an answer for tonight?"

"It's enough," Millie yawned. "For tonight. I expect I will have more questions later."

—From *Millie's Courageous Days*, pages 91–92

Stuart encouraged Millie to practice the virtues of love (found in 1 Corinthians 13) on her friends and family, as well as on her enemies. He said, "But if you really want to see what God can do, practice on your enemies. It takes a lot of work—and courage, too." Once again, God was speaking to Millie about having the courage to love Damaris.

How are you at practicing the virtues of love described in 1 Corinthians 13? Re-read the verse in the above excerpt and jot down the areas you feel you need to improve. Be sure to jot down your areas of strength, too! Be specific.

Areas for Improvement	Areas of Strength

"Poor Damaris," [Marcia] said. "How terribly lonely she must be. Perhaps you can include her in your prayers, Millie."

Can I pray for God to keep her far away from me? Millie was glad that some prayers were private. *Of every soul in Pleasant Plains, Damaris is the only one I cannot grow to like even a little.*

That evening when Millie took out her Bible, the list of family and friends fell out. Her heart tugged at her as she picked it up off the floor. *Have I been practicing loving my family and friends? I've been doing better with the boys. And I have been praying for Rhoda Jane every day. How could I love any better?*

Before she could even think about the answer, her father's words came flooding back to her: *"If you really want to see what God can do, practice on your enemies."*

Millie groaned. "Pappa could not possibly mean that I have to practice love on that horrible Damaris Drybread!" Yet even as the words came out of her mouth, Millie knew that Pappa did mean just that. And so did Jesus. *How can I call myself a Christian if I am not willing to do what I know Jesus wants me to do?*

"It's not possible!" Millie cried, arguing with herself.

But of course it was possible. God had created the stars and the moon. All He had to do to make her love Damaris Drybread was to change Millie's heart.

"I don't want my heart changed! I don't *want* to love her!" exclaimed Millie. But she could not block the words out of her mind: *"It takes a lot of work—and courage, too."*

Millie gritted her teeth and took out her quill. *Damaris Drybread.* She wrote the name quickly at the bottom of her prayer list.

What have I done? She couldn't erase the ink. The name was at the very bottom of the page. All she had to do was tear it off, and it would be gone forever . . . .

Jesus, Millie prayed, *help me want to love her.*

Immediately, she tucked the paper back in her Bible.

—From *Millie's Courageous Days,* pages 184–185

One thing's for sure: Millie needed more than human love when it came to Damaris Drybread! She needed supernatural ("super-natural") love! That's because even thinking about loving Damaris went against everything in Millie's own heart. Yet Millie understood that since she called herself a Christian, she had to be willing to do what Jesus wanted her to do. And she knew that Jesus wanted her to love Damaris Drybread.

A heart willing to embrace the impossible opens itself up to the supernatural love of God. Supernatural love is love we cannot find within ourselves. We tap into God's supernatural love when we tap into God Himself. 1 John 4:7 says, "Dear friends, let us love one another, for love comes from God." In verse 16 it says, "God is love." So if we are lacking in love, we must go to the Source!

Millie could not find love in her own heart for Damaris. To Millie, loving Damaris seemed impossible. But Millie had a heart willing to follow her Lord, despite how she felt about Damaris. So Millie courageously took on the impossible challenge of loving Damaris. How did she do it? It's very simple. She simply "looked to Jesus" (as we learned about earlier) and asked Him to help her *want* to love Damaris. Supernatural love is baffling to the world!

Seeing Through the Eyes of Jesus

The pieces were beginning to come together for Millie. Once she opened her heart to allow Jesus' supernatural love to flow through her, God opened the eyes of Millie's heart and she was able to see the precious life in Damaris—the precious life that God Himself saw in her.

Millie's mind kept going back to Damaris's face. Suddenly she knew where she had seen that look before, hopeless and lost—on Mandy Rose, the day she was left at the Keiths'! A picture of the baby's thin, pinched face flashed through her mind, and Millie almost gasped. *Is that the way You see Damaris, Lord? Someone lost and alone who just needs to be cleaned up and loved? Forgive me for the way I have treated her, Lord.* Even if the fat farmer had not been an angel, God had still sent Mandy Rose to Damaris. He had trusted her to take care of His precious little one until He called her home. *That's what Mamma sees in Damaris! That's what Jesus sees in her.*

At home again, Millie shut the door to her room and took out her writing pad. *Love never fails. Give me the courage to love as You would, Jesus.* She prayed silently, spilling her heart to Jesus, and then began to write:

> *Dear Damaris,*
> *I have not treated you with respect, and I am ashamed of my behavior. I want you to know that I believe God sent Mandy Rose to you because He needed someone to love her. I know you were His very first choice. I hope that someday I can do as good a job of loving and caring for my own child as you did with Mandy.*
> *You said that you have never had a sister. If you will have me, I will be proud to be your sister in Christ.*
>
> *1 Corinthians 13:4,*
> *Millie Keith*

—From *Millie's Courageous Days*, pages 204–205

 **God's supernatural love comes with a bonus — it enables us to see people and circumstances as Jesus sees them!**

What did Millie see in Damaris that she hadn't seen before?

When Millie realized Damaris just needed to be loved, something else happened in Millie's heart. What was her response?

When God allows us to see through His eyes, it is a great, life-changing privilege! But God also gives us another gift — He also allows us to see the waywardness of our own heart. Millie instantly recognized the sin that had darkened her thinking toward Damaris. She felt convicted of the way she had treated Damaris.

 **Being keenly aware of our own sinful heart makes us able to respond to the unlovable characteristics in others with mercy and compassion. Because we desire God to have mercy on us, we need to extend His mercy to others.**

Millie knew that she needed to make things right. She knew in her heart that she had not shown respect toward Damaris. Millie responded in action to the conviction in her heart. She sought to make things right by writing a letter of blessing and encouragement to Damaris. Instead of hoping Damaris would disappear out of her life, Millie now found herself seeking the Lord's supernatural love.

Have you ever felt convicted of the way you treated someone? Describe the situation:

Is there something you need to do to make things right?

The supernatural love that Jesus had for people baffled both His critics and His closest friends! Jesus reached out to all people — from the esteemed rich young ruler to the outcast with leprosy. He had compassion for a woman caught in adultery while the teachers of the law wanted to stone her. He sat and talked with a Samaritan woman when it was a well-known fact that Jews did not associate with Samaritans.

The more you study Jesus' incredible love and compassion for all people, the more your own heart will desire to love as He does.

Look up the following verses:

1) Luke 19:1–10

   a) Write out verse 10:

   b) How did the people react to this encounter with Zacchaeus (see verse 7)?

2) Mark 1:40–42

   a) Write out verse 41:

   b) What attribute of Jesus motivated Him to heal this man?

3) John 8:1–11

    a) Write out verse 7:

    b) Why do you think Jesus' critics left Him and the woman alone (verse 9)?

    c) How did Jesus show supernatural love to the woman?

What did you learn about Jesus from reading the three different Scripture passages?

Jesus had love and compassion toward even the most unlovable of people. When we allow Him to give us His love for someone we can't love on our own, God will do amazing things. Read the following excerpt and see how Millie's adventure with Damaris ends:

> "$\mathcal{G}$et me some more willow bark, Ru," Millie said. As soon as Ru was gone, Millie poured a cup of tea for her Pappa and headed for the stairs. She was so exhausted that she couldn't see straight. The room swam before her eyes. *It is exhaustion, isn't it, Lord? I can't get sick.* The room tilted, and then the cup was on the floor, broken to pieces. Millie was not sure how it had gotten there.
>
> "I need someone to clean that up, God," she said. "I . . . need . . . some help. Send somebody." She felt the room tilt again and knew she was falling, but strangely, she never seemed to hit the ground. Someone's arms were around her and they half led, half carried her to the couch.
>
> "The answer is yes," the arms said.
>
> Millie opened her eyes. "Hello, Damaris. I don't remember the question."
>
> "The question was, whether or not I wanted a sister in Christ. I'm not going to be good at it, I'm sure, but . . . the answer is yes. I've come to help."
>
> — From *Millie's Courageous Days*, pages 217–218

As you can see, the adventure for Millie and Damaris was only just beginning! God not only was doing a work in Millie's heart, helping her to love Damaris, but through Millie's act of lovingkindness toward Damaris, God was able to soften Damaris's heart as well! Now together they would join forces for God's Kingdom instead of becoming greater enemies.

Remember the promise of Proverbs 3:5–6? Write the memory verse below:

Loving people with God's supernatural love means that we must trust God and lean on His understanding, not our own. If Millie leaned on her own understanding of Damaris, she would never have had the courage or inclination to reach out in love. Millie allowed God to change her heart.

You can receive this same supernatural love by simply asking God to change your heart. Your willingness to challenge the impossible will take you on grand adventures of loving as Jesus loved!

 **Remember that it takes courage to love the "Damaris Drybread" in your life. If your heart is willing to open itself to God's supernatural love, God will help you see that person the way He sees them.**

Refer to your past list of people whom you are having a hard time loving (page 168). What might God see in each one that you haven't seen before?

Spend a few minutes in prayer asking God to help you see people and circumstances through His eyes. Humbly ask your Heavenly Father to help you see your own heart as He sees it.

Trusting God for Others' Salvation

*M*illie was glad to get away by herself for a while, climbing up above the festivities. *Is Rhoda Jane's heart ever going to soften, Lord? Is she ever going to want to know more about You? It's bad enough that she won't listen, but she won't let Gordon listen either. It breaks my heart. It must break Yours, too. Help me be the kind of friend who will never give up on her.*

— From *Millie's Courageous Days*, page 88

Millie was heartbroken over Rhoda Jane's hardened heart and the distance that was growing between their friendship. There's nothing worse than having a close friend who constantly rejects God's love for their life. Millie wanted so badly for Rhoda Jane to know God as her own Lord and Savior. Trusting God to love Damaris Drybread was one thing, but now Millie had to learn to trust God with her best friend's salvation!

Do you have a close friend who is rejecting God's love? How does it make you feel?

Millie prayed that God would help her be the kind of friend who would never give up on Rhoda Jane. But as Millie stepped out more in her faith, Rhoda Jane began to reject Millie's friendship!

*R*hoda Jane walked Millie to the door, but her manner was stiff and cold.

"Your mother is able to care for Gordon now," said Millie. "You should come over for tea."

"No," Rhoda Jane said flatly. "I'm sure I have too much to do. And I don't think you should come around here any more. At least not to visit me."

Millie felt as if she had been slapped. "Rhoda Jane, I . . . Why?"

"Because it wasn't fair using religion on Gordon when he was hurt and not thinking straight."

Millie remembered how Rhoda Jane herself had insisted on reading aloud the Bible verse that seemed to help Gordon in his pain and hopelessness. "I didn't *use* religion. God was there for Gordon and —"

"Good-bye, Millie." Rhoda Jane shut the door.

Millie's heart ached as she walked home. *The angels might be having a party, but I am not. I can't bear it! I did and said the things You wanted me to, Lord. But now, I've lost my best friend.*

— From *Millie's Courageous Days*, pages 122–123

Can you imagine what Millie must have felt? She had been obedient to speak the things God told her to speak, and as a result, her best friend wanted nothing to do with her! Once again, what Millie saw was one big mess! Her immediate reaction was to despair. But her mother could sense something was bothering Millie:

"So," Marcia said to Millie when the children ran to play. "Do you want to talk about it?"

"Talk about what, Mamma?"

"Something is troubling you," her mother said. "And it seems to be weighing more heavily on you every day."

Millie sighed. "I don't know that anyone can help me. I miss Rhoda Jane. It's been weeks now, and she hasn't spoken to me."

"I thought that might be it," Marcia said. "God is dealing with Rhoda Jane's heart, and it is very hard for her."

"It's a little hard on me, too," said Millie.

"What do you do when you think of Rhoda Jane?"

"Most of the time I pray for her." Millie pulled up a grass stem and bit it. "Other times I throw rocks in the river, or I scour our pots and pans. Pappa told me once to practice loving my friends as God commands us in the book of Corinthians. But it's hard, Mamma. It hurts to love them when they don't love you back."

"Maybe they do," Marcia said, "and just can't show it because they are hurting, too."

— From *Millie's Courageous Days*, pages 175–176

Marcia saw with eyes of faith — and she was beginning to help Millie see the situation from God's point of view.

How did Marcia encourage Millie?

What did Marcia see about Rhoda Jane that Millie didn't see?

God was dealing with Rhoda Jane's heart. Millie's job wasn't to give up on the friendship or to hound Rhoda Jane into being her friend again. All Millie had to do was to continue to pray and love her friend, even if Rhoda Jane didn't love her back. Love never fails (1 Corinthians 13:7).

Is it hard for you to love a friend who has rejected you? Why?

What have you learned so far from this chapter about trusting God with your relationships?

Our memory verse for this chapter, 2 Corinthians 12:9–10, is a long one. Can you recite it by heart yet? Practice by writing it out here:

As hard as it was, Millie's ultimate desire was to not give up on Rhoda Jane. She wanted to be a friend who could persevere and love, even though no love was being returned. God's faithfulness shined bright in Millie's life! Not only did God do something supernatural when Millie began to love Damaris, but God did it again when Millie trusted God with Rhoda Jane's salvation! Read the wonderful outcome below.

"Well, look who is out of doors!" Rhoda Jane was walking across the yard toward her. "I have been waiting to talk with you, Millie Keith!"

"I have been waiting to talk with you, too," Millie said. "Were you in my room, reading the Bible?"

"Yes," Rhoda Jane said seriously. "That's why I have been waiting for you. I wanted you to hear it first, even before Gordon." Rhoda Jane sat down in the grass and pulled up her knees. "Will you forgive me for shunning you?"

"Of course I will . . ." Millie began, but Rhoda Jane interrupted. "I want to explain. When Gordon became a Christian, I was so angry with you. You were meddling with my family. I thought you had no right. But do you remember when Celestia Ann dared me to ask God for one impossible thing?"

"I don't remember that it was a dare, exactly," Millie said.

Rhoda Jane shrugged. "Well, I asked Him for the most impossible thing I could think of. I asked Him to send Damaris Drybread to my house to say she was sorry for the things she had said and done when my father was dying. It was about five days after Mandy Rose's funeral. Emmaretta was sick, burning with the fever, and Ma was in no shape to help her. I had been watching over her all day when someone knocked at the door. Gordon answered it. I wouldn't have let her in." Rhoda Jane paused a moment, then went on. "Damaris clutched her Bible to her chest. She walked right in, stood in the exact spot she had three years ago . . . and she said she was sorry. She opened her Bible and read to me, all about love. I found the verses later, after she had gone. 'Love is patient, love is kind. It does not envy, it does not boast, it is not proud. . . .' It went on and on and I knew that it was true. The only thing I could think of as she was reading was that I know people who act like that — the Keiths. And now I know why they act like that. Because God is real, and they belong to Him. And I decided I wanted to belong to Him, too — more than anything else on earth. Only I was afraid He wouldn't want me."

"Of course He would!" exclaimed Millie.

"I know. I read the New Testament," Rhoda Jane continued. "Jesus died for me. I want to ask Him to take away my sins, and to be my King. But I waited for you, Millie, because I want you to pray with me."

There were tears in Millie's eyes as they began the prayer of salvation, and tears in Rhoda Jane's before they finished.

— From *Millie's Courageous Days*, pages 219–221

In John 6:44, Jesus says, "No one can come to me unless the Father who sent me draws him."

 **We must rest in God's power for the salvation of others. It is God's work to draw hearts to Him. Our place is to pray in faith for them, to love them unconditionally, and to make sure we are reflecting Jesus in all we say and do.**

Are you trusting God for the salvation of one of your friends? He is faithful and desires to see all people turn to Him. (1 Timothy 2:4) Make a list below of the names of those you want to see saved. Write these names also in a prayer journal and faithfully pray for them that God will draw them to Him. Your prayers are such an important part of this process. Share this list with your parents or other Christian friends so that they can be praying with you.

People I Want to See Saved

Looking Back on the Adventure

> In the year the Keiths had been in Pleasant Plains, a transformation had begun—they were truly becoming a frontier family. Millie's new life was a far cry from the life of privilege she had lived in Lansdale, with servants and shopkeepers ready to provide for her every need. But now she could do things she would never have imagined when she lived in Lansdale: milk a cow, make soap and candles, put up preserves. *I must admit that I do like to learn as much as I can learn, to grow as much as I can grow, and I love being friends with people from every kind of background — just like You were, Jesus.*
>
> —From *Millie's Courageous Days*, page 105

It had only been one short year since Millie left her home in Ohio and joined God in an incredible adventure of trusting Him. Do you remember Millie's first reaction to the news that they were moving to Pleasant Plains? Millie was sure it was a mistake! To her it was a huge disaster to leave her friends and familiar life in Ohio for something new and unknown in Indiana. The process of trusting God through her year-long season of change was a challenge for Millie, but in the end she saw how God had a good plan for her all along.

 **God has a good plan for *your* life — you only need to trust Him. Usually you won't see the big picture of His plan until you look back on your adventure.**

God will produce life-changing fruit in your life as you journey with Him. Millie and her siblings gained many new skills and opportunities to grow as a result of their move to Indiana—skills and opportunities they might never have had if they stayed in Ohio. Not only that, but the spiritual lessons they learned strengthened their faith and resolve to trust in God. The Keith family matured in their relationship with Jesus. God did many, many wonderful things in all of their lives—all in one year!

> "You know, Millie, I am so proud of the way you and Ru—all of you, really—have grown since we moved to the frontier. I can't imagine a boy of Rupert's age taking on the responsibilities he now has back . . ." Millie saw her mother catch herself. She had almost said "back home in Lansdale."

Pleasant Plains is home now, Millie thought. *Really home.* Moving to the frontier had changed the Keiths in many ways. Millie's own hands were sun-browned and rough from helping Ru with the garden and Mamma with the laundry. Mamma served pies made from fruit she had canned herself. Don and Cyril spent most of their time shirtless and barefoot in overalls, although their mother insisted they wear straw hats. They fished with Gordon and spent time with Emmaretta and Min gathering nuts and berries in season. What would her friends in Lansdale think if they could see them now? *I like it, God. It's hard work, but I like it. You did have a good plan.*

—From *Millie's Courageous Days*, pages 172–173

All the hardships, all the tears, and all the lessons learned were worth it for Millie. God taught her so much about His love and His ways through this adventure. Millie learned that God is truly trustworthy, and she learned a lot about living a LIFE of faith!

By finishing this study guide, you too have learned a lot about living a life of faith. You have learned that to trust God, you must:

❖ understand what it means to trust

❖ know God's nature and character—especially His goodness and faithfulness

❖ have a new mindset—the mindset of a "pioneer for God"

❖ know how to hear God's voice and be led by His Holy Spirit

❖ be able to manage your emotions and conquer your bad attitudes

❖ know how to see through eyes of faith, and

❖ let God guide you in your relationships.

God is inviting you on a grand adventure—an adventure with many wonderful surprises along the way.

You cannot begin to imagine the surprises that God has in store for you as you live out your life of faith. But one thing is certain. If you trust in God and faithfully walk in His ways, others will want to come along with you.

" *Someone* very wise once told me that life with God is an adventure," Millie said, "greater and wilder than I could ever imagine. She was right."

"I hope there's room in your adventure for a friend," said Rhoda Jane, sitting on the swing beside Millie. "Because I am coming, too. How high can this thing go?"

—From *Millie's Courageous Days*, page 221

In chapter one, we learned that life is an adventure. You were asked if you liked adventures. Look back over your answers throughout chapter one. Having now completed this study, *Millie's Life Lessons: Adventures in Trusting God*, how do you feel about future adventures with God?

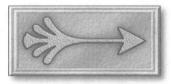

Remember, it takes courage to trust in God because you can't see Him. But the better you know Him, the easier it will be for you to trust Him.

Look back over this chapter. Ask the Holy Spirit to show you the most important things He wants you to remember. Put a star beside those truths and, in your own words, summarize below what He showed you.

Rewrite your thoughts as a prayer, asking God to help you grow and apply the truths He's taught you throughout the chapter.

Write out the memory verse for this chapter, 2 Corinthians 12:9–10:

Write out the memory verse for our entire study, Proverbs 3:5–6:

Your most important and most rewarding adventure in life will be your quest to know God. It's an adventure which will last your lifetime and on into eternity.

Your grand adventure with God is just beginning!

Trust God. He is trust*worthy!*

Do you want to live a life of faith?
Are you interested in having a stronger devotional life?
Millie's Daily Diary can help you!

MILLIE'S DAILY DIARY
A Personal Journal for Girls

SPIRITUAL VITAL SIGNS

When it comes to the human body, vital signs (like your pulse and blood pressure) measure your physical health. Likewise, when it comes to your spiritual health, there are vital signs that measure the state of your spiritual life. Are you walking in faith, hope and love? Are you spending time with God? Are you feeling resentment or hardness of heart toward anyone? Is the fruit of the Spirit growing in you? This is the place to record the results of your regular, spiritual checkups.

Full of beautiful color photos of Millie, this journal has the unique feature of tabbed sections so that entries can be made in different categories — daily reflections, prayers, answers to prayer, favorite Scriptures, goals & dreams, and more.

Available at your local bookstore

Coming Spring 2003:

Coming Christmas 2002:
Millie and Elsie Dolls and Accessories
Watch our web site for details!

Collect all of our Millie Keith Products!

A Life of Faith: Millie Keith

Collect our other
A Life of Faith™ Products!

A Life of Faith: Elsie Dinsmore

Check out
www.alifeoffaith.com

- Get news about Millie and her cousin Elsie
- Find out more about the 19th century world they live in
- Learn to live a life of faith like they do
- Learn how they overcome the difficulties we all face in life
- Find out about Millie and Elsie products
- Join our girls' club

A Life of Faith Books
"It's Like Having a Best Friend From Another Time"

Introducing the Violet Travilla Series!
Coming Spring 2003

If you love Millie and her cousin Elsie, you'll love Violet too!

Violet is creative, sensitive, outgoing, and inquisitive, and her life of faith will inspire you!

Published by Mission City Press
Committed to helping today's girls develop a LIFE of faith!

For more information about
A Life of Faith™ books, dolls, and companion products,
write to Mission City Press, Inc.,
P.O. Box 681913, Franklin, TN 37068-1913,
or call 615-591-1007 or send an email to info@alifeoffaith.com.

Trust in the LORD with all your heart
and lean not on your own understanding;
in all your ways acknowledge him,
and he will make your paths straight.

PROVERBS 3:5–6